TRAGEDY
AND
THE EVENT CONTINUUM

TRAGEDY AND THE EVENT CONTINUUM

J.R. Kantor

1983

The Principia Press

5743 S. Kimbark. Chicago, Illinois 60637

PERMISSION TO QUOTE FROM THE FOLLOWING WORKS

IS GRATEFULLY ACKNOWLEDGED.

A Definition of Tragedy by Oscar Mandel. Copyright (c) 1961 by New York University.

The Death of Tragedy by George Steiner. Copyright (c) 1961 by G. Steiner.

The Origins of Psychoanalysis by Sigmund Freud. Copyright (c) 1954 by Basic Books.

Tragedy and Philosophy by Walter Kaufmann. Copyright (c) 1958 by Doubleday.

ISBN 0911188-35-5

5743 S. Kimbark Ave.
Chicago, Illinois 60637

CONTENTS

PREFACE

Numerous tragedies of various sorts are constant and significant events in the realm of nature as in that of human situations. But this circumstance goes unnoticed by scholars with the result that the human type of tragedy is usually regarded as the exclusive form. Hence, the consequent misinterpretation of the nature and significance of the tragic aspects of the entire continuum of events.

Furthermore, the literature concerned with human tragedy is largely confined to the dramatic representation of personal relations though theatrical plays are only ambiguous imitations of the anthropic type of events. In effect, the study of the essentially tragic is shunted to a narrow side track which prevents a proper appreciation of a unique and important type of variants in the continuum of happenings.

Even more disturbing is that plays that do simulate human events, that is dramas in general, are described in terms of folk wisdom, unscientific psychology, inauthentic philosophy, as well as questionable moral and religious principles. Obviously then, for an adequate understanding of tragic events, both in nature and in culture, a broad and precise intellectual horizon is essential. The following interrelated factors from the event continuum require analysis and interpretation.

A. TRAGEDY AS MOMENTOUS EVENTS IN NATURE.

Examples, earthquakes, mudslides, droughts, floods, conflagrations, and so on. These are happenings based on cosmic and telluric conditions. When human beings are affected, that is only incidental to the total situation.

B. TRAGEDY AS HUMAN EVENTS.

Examples, individual pathologies, malformations, poverty, deaths, as well as group destructions, wars, and many other disastrous occurrences. No sensitive person can fail to be profoundly impressed by individual and group behavior which represents the apparent reversion of human beings to a lower stage of evolution. Fundamentalism flourishes and challenges thinking and its freedom. The achievements of hominids over the centuries are retreated from. Persons and their governments are poised for the destruction of entire enemy populations. National and international relations now include the seizure and assassination of prominent persons in local and in unfriendly nations. Within presumably civilized communities the practice of individual torture is commonplace. Parents are made to witness the torture of their children and vice versa. Wars and the threats of wars interfere with the general well-being of the citizenry of all communities. Disharmonies, strife, and terror everlastingly dominate the atmosphere of civil living. The discoveries and general achievements of scientific research and the perfections of technology are put to the sordid purposes of destruction and slaughter.

C. TRAGEDY AS PUTATIVE REPRESENTATIONS OF HUMAN CIRCUMSTANCES.

Examples, plays, dramas, novels, and other literary productions.

All these, including the acts of describing and explaining any of the happenings mentioned, are all points in the continuum of events.

THE SCIENTIFIC APPROACH

In the present essay, tragic events as well as events in general are studied by the methods obtaining in all scientific investigation, that is, by analysis and description of confrontable event fields and their auspicive conditions, with minimum influence from established beliefs and traditions. We submit that a naturalistic outlook upon events of nature and of culture casts considerable light upon phenomena of all types and the way they should be described and interpreted.

TWO SCIENTIFIC GUIDE LINES

1. THE PRINCIPLE OF SPECIFICITY. Among the basic guide lines of scientific work is the specificity principle which directs the analyzing of the particular components and traits of things and events, both as unique systems and as related to other systems of objects and events. It is such analyses that reveal the similarities and variations of particular objects and events whether in nature or culture, as well as the validity of the observations and descriptions of objects and events.

2. THE PRINCIPLE OF RELEVANT FACTORS. Another basic guide line is an appreciation of the cultural and intellectual climate surrounding the interpretation of events. With respect to tragic events, it is imperative to acknowledge the continuity in events of nature and culture and not be misled by the hominid paranoia that human events are basically different from the other members of the event continuum. Homo Mensura is not a general criterion for what is or is not tragedy.

TRAGEDY AND TRIUMPH

Finally, it is impossible to overlook that the miseries and disappointments of human living have their counterpart in the improvements and gains of homo sapiens. Tragedies covary with conquest. Unquenchable is the flame of light and reason which partially illuminates the surrounding darkness. Not only is homo faber stretching out his technogy to reach the planets of distant space, but one can discern the embryonic development of a reasonable philosophy and an authentic science that mark a great advance in knowledge and civilization. Advancements in psychology and philosophy afford hope that new light may be cast upon the problems of tragedy as well as the entire event continuum.

October, 1982 J.R.K.

CHAPTER I

TRAGEDY AS EVENTS AND AS DRAMATIC DEPICTION

Tragic events, whatever name they bear or how they are described, occupy a very large place among the innumerable happenings in the realms of nature and of culture. And yet such events, as momentous as they may be, receive scant consideration as compared with other types of events. Not that there are lacking many library shelves with the word "tragedy" printed on the books that weigh them down. However, a close look at the literature on tragedy reveals that the subject they treat is primarily plays, compositions for theatrical show, not events in nature and in the lives of individuals and their societies. In brief, various styles of literary dramas dominate the thinking and the productions of those interested in literary compositions.

By contrast, the present study belongs to the relatively sparse class of investigations devoted to the analysis of tragic events, whether immediately observed or known through literary interpretations of tragic circumstances. It represents an attempt to elucidate the nature and conditions of a specific type of event based on the naturalistic postulates recently developed in science and scientific philosophy. The target of the present investigation is a synthesis built upon the observation of actually occurring events as well as a consideration of the variant ways they have been intellectually treated.

Probably the first requirement for such a study is to acknowledge some distinctions within the general domain of events as in the following schema.

SCHEMA OF EVENT TYPES

1. PRISTINE EVENTS, that is occurrences or happenings whether (a) known or unknown, (b) controllable or not controllable, or (c) conventionally classified as inorganic, organic, or humanistic. Obvious telluric and cosmic examples are such things as (a) stars, planets, mountains, rivers, soil, plants, metals, (b) processes as earthquakes, floods, snows, organic births and deaths, and (c) the innumerable behaviors of persons or groups in their cultural organizations and practices.

The primary significance of the term "pristine" is to emphasize the lack of intrusion of any human dependence upon the existence of this class of events. Consequently, there is excluded all metaphysical beliefs about psychic creations of things and events as to their existence, or acquaintance should they become known.

The assumption of no independently existing things and events is, of course, founded upon the traditional epistemological and metaphysical postulate that things exist only by virtue of mental projection. The nonobjective principle appears acceptable to many persons because of the confusion between occurrences as over against the reactions to the qualities and properties of things and events. Naturally, the perceiving and knowing of things is bountifully furnished with assumptions from the experiences of knowers. But just as certainly is authentic knowledge based upon the qualities of things whose existence precedes the knowing by many time units of some sort, even by aeons of light years.

Perceiving, knowing, and believing events are invariably interbehaviors of organisms with preexisting objects, events, conditions, and other organisms. In the case of believing, of course, there must be substitute objects.[1]

A ray of light may be thrown upon pristine events by the consideration that telluric and cosmic events are merely the most distant from human circumstances located on the continuum, whereas events involving hominid factors constitute less remote happenings than purely inorganic things and events.

2. ORGANISMIC EVENTS. For our present purpose, a special type of events may be made of the behavior of organisms, especially human beings. The latter may or may not be subject to or under control of other individuals. Here may be listed all the things and events comprised in the contacts of organisms and persons with other organisms, persons, objects, conditions, and results. Here is the grand domain of human endeavor, creation, failure, decline, and progress, whether personal or societal. The number of such events are so numerous and so varied as to thwart specification. It is sufficient, however, to mention the records of the encounters as they are available in the experiences and histories of persons, the advice in the how-to books, and in the handbooks of all the sciences.

3. LITERARY EVENTS. Plays, dramas, and literature in general and their production make up a special type of events. Steiner asserts that "all men are aware of tragedy in life. But tragedy in the form of drama is not universal."[2] Of course, not all people are concerned with theatrical affairs, but plays as written, performed, and criticised constitute a large sector of humanistic events. What is lacking is a professional and

1. Cf. Kantor, J.R., *Principles of Psychology,* Chicago, Principia, 1924, 1926, and Kantor, J.R. and Smith, N.W., *The Science of Psychology: An Interbehavioral Survey,* Chicago, Principia, 1975
2. Steiner, G., *The Death of Tragedy,* New York, Knopf, 1961, p. 3.

technical concern for tragical events. Followers of the literary criticism tradition frequently raise the question whether or not a dramatic production is a genuine tragedy, though few scholars might question the authenticity of the Greek and Shakespearean tragedies, as do Richards[3] and Abel.[4]

Such problems cannot be raised about actually occurring behavior events and circumstances. What may be disagreed upon is the naming of events. While events are what they are, constructions as hypotheses or theories may vary greatly on the basis of the constructor's background and experience as well as upon the criteria he uses or is imposed upon him.

OBSERVATION AND INTERPRETATION OF EVENTS

Tragic events in some form have quite expectedly captured the interest of philosophers, literary scholars and others, yet it is evident that the subject still needs clarification on the basis of a naturalistic appreciation of people, their works, circumstances, and their general joyful and sorrowful experiences as well as inordinate conditions and changes in nature.

For the most part, literary scholars have been interested in the problem of attitudes or general psychological reactions to tragedy but have not sufficiently analyzed the nature of tragedy as a type of occurring events. Philosophers, of course, have paid considerable attention to the nature of tragedy as reflected in dramatic episodes but have not been well enough equipped with naturalistic attitudes to do justice to tragedy as occurring events. Actually, they have intermixed with their descriptions religious and moral views verbally formulated without relation to observation.

It is one of the fundamental features of the present work to make clear the difference between dramas and tragic events. Dramas or plays are constructions and not pristine,

3. Richards, I.A., *Principles of Literary Criticism*, London, Kegan Paul, 1928, p. 247.
4. Abel, L., *Metatheatre: A new view of dramatic form*, New York, Hill and Wang, 1963, p. 5.

that is independently existing, events. They are, as it were, secondary events, and carry the premises and forms that are traditional or idiosyncratically invented. Of course, dramas may point to or represent authentic tragedies, but on the whole, they partake in the transcendent traits of religious and mythical institutions. In general, the writers in the dramatic traditions employ the words "tragic" and "tragical" in a casual way with little regard to any very specific referents as contents.

Kitto[5] has compared the interpretation of Aeschylus' *Oresteia* by Kuhns[6] with that of Jones.[7] The former believes that "the terrible punishment meted out to Cassandra is the result of yet another violation of the marriage vows and female duty... In breaking her word and denying her duty, Cassandra has violated the covenant of marriage ...." Jones, on the other hand, declared that "gods and men alike are assailed by the erotic feeling, by the same blend of physical itch and more exalted elements which assail humans, " and it was this that "caused Apollo to attempt the rape of Cassandra."

Here it is clearly pointed out that it is not the difference in writers or literary critics, nor the variations in texts, but rather that plays are constructions and not pristine events of nature, so like the ambiguous figures of elementary psychology, can provide occasions for variations of interpretation.

Dramas, like all artistic creations, are properly treated by critics as things. Thus they may pass judgment upon the structure of plays. They may ask if the various depictive factors are congruous or incongruous, if they are properly constructed in verse or prose. Another critical approach is to ask about the competence of the author and the effects produced on the audiences. A very important problem is to ask why

5. Kitto, H.D.F., *Poiesis, Structure and Thought*, Berkeley, University of California Press, 1966, p. 5.
6. Kuhns, R., *The House, the City and the Judge*, Indianapolis, Merrill, 1962, p. 40.
7. Jones, J., *On Aristotle and Greek Tragedy*, New York, Oxford University Press.

plays are attended even when they are concerned with the distasteful acts of murder, destruction, antimoral, or obscene happenings. Since critics are free to say that it is a matter of amusement, a play is to enjoy, attendance at tragedies is a form of play, thus supporting Huzinga in his insistence that audiences are made up of Homo Ludens, as in most human affairs.[8]

Dramatic plays are far from pristine tragic events insofar as they have to be limited to human situations. Moreover, since dramas are intended to please audiences or to conform to standardized patterns, they cannot serve well, if at all, for the appreciation of the essential components of tragic events.

How different theatrical plays are from pristine events is strikingly demonstrated in the numerous criticisms of the structures and significances of dramas. As critical analysts say, the variant interpretations of the details of plays are simply opinions, and it is even said that there is little similarity between the interpretations and the text. Now if this situation were corrected, it would only provide a correspondence between the interpretation and the text, but no sort of relationship between texts and pristine events that the texts are supposed to represent.

SPECIALIZED APPROACHES TO TRAGIC EVENTS

Tragic events being omnipresent and extremely impelling, it is to be expected that observers and interpreters should develop varying attitudes toward such occurrences. Although many attitudes reflect glaring insufficiencies, the scanning of them is helpful for the process of developing a valid view, and discarding views based on inadequate psychological and philosophical premises. To scan such an enormous collection

8. Huzinga, J., *Homo Ludens: A Study of the Play Element in Culture*, London, Routledge, 1949.

of views, severe selective procedure is unavoidable. Accordingly, we limit our examination to the following five attitude areas.

1. Literary Criticism.
2. Philosophical Perspectives.
3. Moral Standpoints.
4. Religious Institutions.
5. Psychological Circumstances.

LITERARY CRITICISM. Views in this class, whether applicable or nonapplicable to tragic events, follow traditional patterns. For the most part, plays center about the misfortunes of certain persons involved in circumstances arranged by their authors. The general formula used is the death of a hero, or at least an unhappy ending to the particular circumstances depicted on the stage. For example, the conditions presumed to give character and interest to dramas depend upon the goodness or the popularity of the hero protagonist and the intensity of the sufferings that the author can bestow upon him.

As we indicate in Chapter III, the attitudes of playwrights depend upon the cultural conditions of their time, so that Greek plays differ in content and form from those of later periods. But in each period, different authors produce pattern variations on the basis of the circumstances attending their unique experiences including their development of philosophical, psychological, and religious attitudes. These attitudes will, of course, influence their dramatic products. Thus playwrights may or may not include comic relief, indicate their motivation whether writing as artists, or for profits, to please theatre goers and so on. Their products, too, may more or less resemble actual situations.

PHILOSOPHICAL PERSPECTIVES. Philosophers of many persuasions have felt free to characterize tragic situations of whatever sort they treated. For the most part, the generalized theme they employ is loss or destruction of some thing or circumstance of value, death, agony, suffering, or evil in the world. Although in many instances, the views presented may be criticized as too general or too limited, still some feature of actual tragic events are referred to in their formulations.

A prominent example is the empathy view of Lipps who proposes that how a tragic event appears to an onlooker depends upon the way one feels into it. The affect of an art object, say a tragedy, is influenced by the sophisticated insight experienced concerning its nature and conditions of being. Thus the deaths of Antigone and Desdemona may not be tragic as compared with the death of Romeo.[9]

Philosophical perspectives may be categorized as pessimistic or optimistic. Of course, the former type of view is the most evident. A good example of the pessimistic attitude is that of Schopenhauer. This is indicated in the following:

> Tragedy is to be regarded, and is recognised as the summit of poetical art, both on account of the greatness of its effect and the difficulty of its achievement. It is very significant for our whole system, and well worthy of observation, that the end of this highest poetical achievement is the representation of the terrible side of life. The unspeakable pain, the wail of humanity, the triumph of evil, the scornful mastery of chance, and the irretrievable fall of the just and innocent, is here presented to us; and in this lies a significant hint of the nature of the world and of existence. It is the strife of will with itself, which here, completely unfolded at the highest grade of its objectivity, comes into fearful prominence. It becomes visible in the suffering of men, which is now introduced, partly through chance and error, which appear as the rulers of the world, personified as fate, on account of their insidiousness, which even reaches the appearance of design; partly it proceeds from man himself, through the self-mortifying efforts of a few, through the wickedness and perversity of most.[10]

9. Lipps, T., *Der Streit über die Tragodie*, Hamburg urd Leipzig, Voss, 1891.
10. Schopenhauer, A., *The World as Will and Idea*, London, Kegan Paul, 1907, p. 326.

Attitudes toward tragedy may be sums of sentimentality as long as one is preoccupied with anthropic situations. But one is constrained to propose a multiple description that embraces both anthropic and nonanthropic situations. The formula then reads, Tragedy is a situation in which authentic potentialities are cut off by untoward circumstances. This formula comprises all the variables that can be deduced from the tragic complex and made into a component of a view or theory of tragedy.

While the great majority of views, theories, and assumptions about the nature of tragedy stem from the domain of literature, both the writers of tragedies and the commentators thereof must be revealing ideas that have some relevance to tragic events.

Plays for Aristotle are imitations of actions which viewed by the audience serves to relieve them of the troublesome actions of pity and fear. The obvious shortcomings of Aristotle's theory are that there are so many restrictions. First, he limits tragedy to the initiation of only two types of feeling, next he restricts tragedy to stage imitations of actions, moreover he adopts a therapeutic aspect to characterize tragedy. There simply is not a large enough canvas to depict so complex and so important a type of events. Still Aristotle's views of tragedy have set the pace for a gigantic literature.

A number of other specific suggestions as basic descriptions of tragedy have been offered, not all focussed on plays or theatre experience. A very prominent theory of this sort is the emphasis upon death, though minor variations depart from simply death as such but specify it must be the death of a hero or some outstanding character. Proponents of this suggestion realize, of course, that just death is hardly a tragic occurrence because of its universal inevitability.

A variant of this proposal is to assume that the essence of tragedy is the finality and irrevocability of death. This addition appears to verify the importance of death as a human trait and opens the way to the evaluation of death as a universal calamity.

From philosphic sources comes a general view of tragedy and one that relates to the lives of persons in general. It is the view of Kallen, who proposes that tragedy is the destruction of value while the destroyer too must be an excellence. The formula for the essential nature of tragedy is the loss of value by value. Although there is considerable merit in Kallen's qualifying the weight of a loss since that implies conditions and substantiality to situations called tragic, there still seems a lessening of the magnitude of the situation. The balancing of the loss by gain is significant.

Another example of a philosophical view of tragedy that appears valid in the light of both artifactual and authentic conditions of life may be referred to as the curtailment of potentialities. In effect, the theory holds that the poignancy of human tragic situations lies in the breakdown or change of circumstances whereby an authentic potentiality of some sort becomes unavailable or lost. In nonanthropic situations a drought, a turbulence below the surface of the earth destroys existing conditions of significance to the world of things and events which may or may not involve human beings.

MORALISTIC PRINCIPLES. The form and shape of intellectual attitudes, whether general viewpoints, theories, explanations, or basic assumptions are invariably faint echoes of deeply intrenched institutions that support the essential structures of given cultures. However, few operate so conspicuously as the intellectual attitudes of morality or religious faith that dominate the thinking about tragic events. There are definite trends in the general adherence to the anthropic character of tragic events as well as the power resident in moralistic situations and in ethnic faiths.

As we should expect, theories of tragedy or viewpoints about tragic situations are hardly ever limited to a single aspect. Accordingly, the theories and views in this class may coincide closely with the proposals made under the philosophical heading. Problems are suggested about good and evil as pertaining to the hero or what he is doing in the plot of the play. Also, the themes of justice, punishment, retribution, resignation, and so on play a part in the activities presented on the stage.

Prominent among the moralistic considerations of writers on tragedy is the problem of unjust suffering, a theme which aids the transition to the following specialized approach to tragic events, that of religion.

RELIGIOUS INSTITUTIONS. Religious conceptions of tragedy imply at the outset the ubiquitous presence of a deity or some personal or impersonal power that is governing or misgoverning the persons involved in general tragic situations. Questions are at once raised as to how and why a beneficent being would permit the deterioration and moral decline of persons and their acts. How could a good and just god permit the existence of destruction and losses of personality, character, and general upheavals of tragic situations?

The domain of religion that is relevant to tragedy study is sharply divided between those who insist that tragedy is only a condition of conflict and disharmony within a great absolute or supreme being and those who deny the compatibility of a compassionate god with evil and destruction. The opposition here stems from assuming different points of vantage. Those scholars who do not assume religious notions as immediately basic to all existence and thinking believe there is an uncrossable barrier between religion and tragedy. The following statements are typical.

> Christian salvation opposes tragic knowledge. The chance of being saved destroys the tragic sense of being trapped without chance of escape. Therefore no genuinely Christian tragedy can exist.[11]

11. Jaspers, K., *Tragedy is Not Enough*, London, Gollancz, 1953, p. 38.

> Tragedy is only possible to a mind which is for the moment agnostic or Manichean. The least touch of any theology which has a compensating Heaven to offer the tragic hero is fatal.[12]

Professor Raphael[13] devotes a large part of his book to the problem of religion and tragedy and assumes a negative attitude. He brings to light the view of Dr. Chu[14] who makes excellent comparisons of the cultures of the East and West to indicate the divergence between religion and tragedy.

In all prevailing intellectual approaches to tragedy, we can observe either dimly or clearly the lack of analysis and investigation such as is practised in various scientific enterprises carried out under naturalistic circumstances. In depictions of tragedy, there is prominent a definite aura of abstractionism, universalism, and autistic opinion. It is as though the occurrence and character of tragic situations are not based on events, observation, and analysis, but simply upon tradition. So far as theory or viewpoints are concerned, all is tragic gloom and unfathomable darkness. There are two fundamental conditions for this situation. In the first place, dramatic plays are the bases of the views, and secondly, the interest in tragedy arises from a religious matrix.

LUX EX RES

And yet out of this dank darkness appear rays of light, some components of valid description become discernible. This is a circumstance arising from the very nature of tragic situations. Decline and destruction are noted, losses of value are seen, inevitability and suffering force themselves upon the attention of observers, and so both participants and spectators of tragic scenes contribute to the description of tragic events.

---

12. Richards, I.A., *Principles of Literary Criticism*, London, Kegan Paul, 1928, p. 246.
13. Raphael, D.D., *The Paradox of Tragedy*, London, Allen and Unwen, 1960.
14. Chu, Kwang-Tsien, *The Psychology of Tragedy*, Strasbourg, Librairie de Universitaire d'Alsace, 1933.

It must be admitted that the very nature of viewpoint requires much reflection and critical analysis. To begin with, of course, views are constructions developed by individuals who are more or less closely in contact with the types of situations and events that they are indicating or describing. Valid attitudes as over against autistic speculation are always based on a capable and critical evaluation of persons, characters, and situations. It follows then that contact with all sorts of tragic situations must be available both in what we have called anthropic and nonanthropic types.

PSYCHOLOGICAL CIRCUMSTANCES. Even though tragedy study is mainly taken to be the analysis and criticism of plays or literary constructions about people, it is not surprising that psychological circumstances should be prominent factors in the literature on tragedy. It is on this pretext that scientific problems should be included among the specialized approaches to tragedy. However, it must be said at once that no scientific treatment of philosophy is as yet available, nor is the psychology that is dragged in for description or interpretation either scientific or authentic with respect to tragic events.

Attitudes toward tragical situations based on psychological premises are in a most unsatisfactory condition. Conventional psychological premises are founded upon invalid traditional thinking. Briefly, tragic events are described and interpreted on the basis of animistic inner processes of soul or mind. None of the constructions are derived from human events but from traditional theories developed in ancient times. Writers who attempt to account for the undesirable and violent behavior in tragic situations resort to such abstractions as spiritistic feelings, emotions, intellectual operations, and so on. The credibility of such imaginary entities exists only because they have been absorbed into folklore and what is generally known as popular psychology.

An especially striking example of a mythical psychological description and explanation of tragic events is the Freudian identification of mythical psychology with the Sophoclean rendering of the Oedipus invention. The following quotation from Freud's letter to Wilhelm Fliess clearly shows the circular process of beginning with a mythical play and transforming a description of it into a universal theory to explain the original myth.

> I have found love of the mother and jealousy of the father in my own case too, and now believe it to be a general phenomenon of early childhood, even if it does not always occur so early as in children who have been made hysterics. (Similarly with the "romanticization of origins" in the case of paranoiacs- heroes, founders of religion.) If that is the case, the gripping power of *Oedipus Rex*, in spite of all the rational objections to the inexorable fate that the story presupposes, becomes intelligible, and one can understand why later fate dramas were such failures. Our feelings rise against any arbitrary, individual fate such as shown in the *Ahnfrau*, etc., but the Greek myth seizes on a compulsion which everyone recognizes because he has felt traces of it in himself. Every member of the audience was once a budding Oedipus in phantasy, and this dream-fulfillment played out in reality causes everyone to recoil in horror, with the full measure of repression which separates his infantile from his present state.[15]

Clear it certainly is that the Freudian psychology is compounded entirely of fantastic notions of human events plus ingredients derived from mythological sources. To begin with, Freud follows in the footsteps of traditional dualism which dichotomizes persons into two aspects, the organismic and the psychic, the latter existing outside spatio-temporal boundaries. Such mythological psychology easily associates with literary mythology.

Despite the fact that psychoanalysis is neither psychology nor science, it still has many defenders and promoters. Kermode[16] believes that analysts of literary texts have much to learn from the mythology of psychoanalysis. In Green's

15. Freud, S., *Letters*, New York, Basic Books, 1954, p. 223 f.
16. Kermode, F., Foreword to Green, A., *The Tragic Effect*, Cambridge, University Press, 1979.

texts[17] one meets with numerous analysts who have practised their scholarship on dramatic problems, for example, Lacon, Delcourt, Winnicott, and other practitioners of psychoanalytic hermeneutics.

---

17. Green, A., *The Tragic Effect,* Cambridge, University Press, 1979.

CHAPTER II

POSTULATION FOR THE STUDY OF TRAGEDY

To be successful in the study of tragedy, it is essential as in all valid investigations to be alert to the problem of basic assumptions. This precaution is not only necessary for the avoidance of preconceptions, but also to be critical and properly selective in choice of materials to be worked upon, plus the entire operational methodology. Probably the most striking example of building upon inadequate postulates is the age-old vogue of Euclidean geometry with its absolute assumptions that space is rectilinear, and triangle sums always 180°. Modern geometry and the evolution of modern science are not merely a matter of suitable techniques and operations, but beyond that, an increased awareness of postulation problems and their control. In the following paragraphs, we present the assumptions marking the intellectual foundations of our study.

THE EVOLUTIONAL BACKGROUND

In the present work, the basic assumptions are invariably evolutional. Whether we concern ourselves with tragedy in the spheres of nature or in culture, we are dealing with events having definite origins in prior phases of things and conditions and which form a basis for future circumstances. These considerations apply to situations in which persons may or may not be involved, or if present, the human events may be partially involved or stand in the center of tragic situations. In any case, when tragic events are seen in perspective, they are taken to be culminating factors in a system that began with the origin of an inorganic astronomical complex called a galaxy, which then gave origin to organismic things and events and ended up with the psychological and general cultural worlds. The accompanying diagram suggests the process. In each period, the specific events have developed through their particular conditions. Each period belongs in its successive place following the earliest origins of the inorganic things and events. While the origin of the earth may be estimated to having been formed billions of years ago, the origin of mankind dates only from about three millions of years. The development of the earth may be traced back to a period when only hydrogen was present from which developed first helium and then all the other numerous elements which later combined to produce all the objects existing from the vast reaches of time until the present. What is to be properly assumed is that innumerable plethoras of simple and complex events have taken place in the historical succession. Furthermore, the indefinitely large number of unit happenings have occurred in relation with others from the earliest time to this. So the earliest inorganic or physiochemical events are continuous with the organic evolution of all plants and animals and beyond to include mankind.

NATURALISTIC ATTITUDE

The evolutional assumption or postulate strictly carried out guarantees that tragedy study will be fully naturalistic and will exclude mysterious processes and entities. All descriptions and interpretations will be treated on the basis of things and events actively occurring in systematic relationships with other things and conditions. On this basis, we can avoid the numerosity of opinions about the variables to be discovered in tragic situations.

A naturalistic viewpoint is of great service in appreciation of the great prevalence and domination of the Aristotelian emphasis of two reactions to tragic drama, namely pity and fear. To the observation of these two reactions, the study of tragedy, whether humanistic or nonhumanistic, will reveal many more types of behavior. But just as important will be a more scientific understanding of philosophy in all its aspects touching upon problems of tragedy.

EVENTS AND CONSTRUCTIONS

An extremely important postulate for intellectual workers is a clear appreciation of the difference between events and reactions to them. By this postulate, we are warned to keep separate and distinct events that we investigate from the intellectual constructions or reactions such as beliefs, descriptions, and theories or viewpoints.[1] For example, in the present context, we must be alert to the subject matter we are studying, whether tragedy is an event in nature, in literature and drama, or powers or entities which hover over the activities and interrelations of people to bring about calamities, deaths, injuries, errors, and misbehaviors.

LINGUISTIC LIMITATIONS

The great importance of careful attention to assumptions is shown in the respect for the ambiguities and limitations of language. Because of the limited vocabulary in use for discussing tragedy problems and analyzing poetic and dramatic works, there is much room for ambiguities, falsification, incorrect, inadequate, and irrelevant notions. An example,

1. For an extended exposition of problems of events and constructions, see Kantor, J.R., *The Logic of Modern Science*, Chicago, Principia, 1953.

when the term "tragedy" is employed, it is imperative to be certain that one is referring to an event or nothing at all. It is basically a linguistic problem that confuses words with things or events. In general, alertness to the identities of (a) direct interbehavior with things and persons, and (b) the situations in which one interbehaves with stimulus objects indirectly as when the latter are described, evaluated, or interpreted. Thus when plays are staged, monologue, dialogue, and asides contribute so much to the performance. In general, the linguistic postulate forces upon the student of tragedy the exceptionless point that the essence of some tragedies and the attitudes toward them are only reactions or behavior of persons as participants or as spectators and as such, can only be properly dealt with by adequate identification.

Finally, it may be said that alertness to basic postulation is a necessary preface for a full appreciation of the goal of investigation and the manner in which the investigation is carried out. This applies to the study of tragedy as to any other subject matter.

CHAPTER III

HISTORICAL SUCCESSION IN TRAGEDY STUDY

TRAGEDY IN THE THEATRE

Considerable light is cast upon all problems pertaining to events whether natural or artifactual by glancing over the records of tragedy study. The records show clearly a threefold variation in the way events are believed to occur and are interpreted. These variations are designated as the (a) Objective Greek Period, (b) the Post Greek Spiritistic Period, and (c) a Current Objective Period. These periods, of course, reflect the culture of various collectivities with continuities and conversions as developed by the historical experiences of individuals and societies. We consider these periods in the order of time both for dramas and for tragic events. First we examine the drama situation, leaving the views concerning general tragic events to later chapters.

THE GREEK OBJECTIVE REACTION TO PLAYS

As in all matters touching nature or culture, it is to Aristotle that we must turn to learn about the origin and interest of research traditions. This is no less the case in tragic situations than in many others. Aristotle as the master of all who know has taken the world of tragedy study in his train although his ideas pertain mostly to tragedy in dramatic stage versions. His enormous influence in the field has been dramatically pictured in the following quotation.

There is something Roman about Aristotle. He has not soared into immortality with the bright grace of the Greek; he has conquered it, province by province, with the resolution, the monumental strength, the practical good sense of Rome. Long after the ancient world has fallen into ruin, the ways his thought had paved still guided the medieval mind amid the thickets of its theology; just as the Roman roads ran on across the wasted lands where the eagles had yielded place to the raven and the crow. And as, even today, when we whirl along our highways, we still cannot go far without following or crossing some undeviating vestige of the march of Rome, so beneath many lines of modern thought endure the foundations laid by the master of Alexander the Great.[1]

An analysis of Aristotle's *Poetics* shows that for Aristotle a tragedy (play) is an imitation of a serious and weighty action, that is, a drama must portray some sort of event observed or invented. It is assumed that the invention resembles elements of an actual situation, but only at a remote point.

The First Essential, The Life and Significance Of Tragedy Is Action.[2]

For Aristotle a play is an event- an imitation or representation, an object-product of a poet or playwright. He describes the context or structure with details of the factors. These are listed as spectacle, character, fable, diction, melody, and thought. Of the six elements of a play, the most important is the fable or plot while the others are enhancing accessories. It is the plot or action that represents living, happiness, and misery.[3] The characters or personalities of the actors are secondary factors. They provide quality but not action. Aristotle's behavioral attitudes shine through all his analyses and pronouncements.

---

1. Lucas, F.L., *Tragedy: Serious Drama in Relation to Aristotle's Poetics*, London, Hogarth Press, 1927, p. 11.
2. Aristotle, *Poetics*, 1450^a, 39.
3. Aristotle, *Poetics*, 1449^b, 17.

When Aristotle characterizes plays as imitations, he intends to stress action as what the play is all about. Also that the play is a fable and not an event as are events in nature. But of course, it is hardly necessary to point out that plays are poetry, natural events though not events of pristine nature.

Throughout the *Poetics*, Aristotle displays his naturalistic and pragmatic attitudes. This is shown by his specification of the place of the spectators. Tragedies must contain incidents which arouse in on-lookers the affective behavior of pity and fear. It is the practical result of viewing some horrible stage behavior that the aroused pity and fear should serve the therapeutic purpose of purging such behavior.

Again, the concrete nature of plays is demonstrated by the provision that the diction or language medium of the actors should be attractive or provide pleasure to the spectators though the language must not be narration, but rather the actors must dramatize the imitated action.

As intimated, literary tragedy study comprises two aspects, (a) presented events, and (b) behavior of persons as spectators at artifactual stage presentations. Though stage spectacles are involved with possible features of tragic events by way of content, form, and structure, they must be kept sharply separated from pristine tragic events. This is especially the case since tragic dramas are based on specialized types of humanistic tragedies, whether veritable or imitations.

Since scholarship pertaining to tragedy either follows Aristotelian pronouncements, comments upon them or deviates from them, it is well to review his treatise entitled *De Poetica.*

As a Greek of the prechristian era and as an experimental biologist, Aristotle looked upon literary tragedies in a straightforward naturalistic manner, as in all of his thinking and writing. In the present context, of course, he emphasizes poetry instead of pristine tragic events. Aristotle's objective viewpoint is indicated by the prominence he accords the psychological question of why people enjoy the horrors of tragic plays. His universally famous answer is the purgation of the affective states of pity and fear. Rather than objecting to the therapeutic aspects of tragedy spectatorship as does Lucas when he asserts that the theatre is not a hospital,[4] it is more historical and significant to emphasize the practicality, the pragmatic reality of confrontable tragic situations. These aspects of tragic performances Aristotle sums up in his well known statement in his *Poetics.*

> A tragedy, then, is the imitation of an action that is serious and also, as having magnitude, complete in itself; in language with pleasurable accessories, each kind brought in separately in the parts of the work; in a dramatic, not in a narrative form; with incidents arousing pity and fear, wherewith to accomplish its catharsis of such emotions.[5]

In addition to the long line of literary critics, philosophers of various times and places have built up a tradition of interpretations on the basis of cultural attitudes available at the time. Those views range from explanations of moral and religious elements to solutions of pseudo-psychological propositions. Both the literary critics and the philosophers have confined tragic events to the human type of situation. Most of the time the views expressed departed widely from actual situations in favor of the constantly recurring remarks concerning good and evil and the question whether a deity would subject the worthy and faithful to the utmost suffering even when excellent compensation was later allotted as in the case of the Biblical story of Job.

In accord with the objective philosophy of the Greek period, the tragedians were formal and impersonal. This is shown by the concentration upon legends, mythology, and general cultural abstractions, like fate and the various gods,

4. Lucas, F.L., *Tragedy,* New York, Harcourt Brace, 1928, p. 31.
5. Ross, W.D. (ed.), *The Student's Oxford Aristotle,* Vol. 6, 1449^b, 23.

erinys, and demons. While the plots or actions ultimately had to be derived from human behavior, the stress was upon the ideal and moral institutions. Antigone bewailed her conventionally virginal death more than her personal demise.

Writers on classical tragedy study consider that Aristotelian poetics are in a sense correctives for the views of his teacher Plato. But this is not necessarily the case. Rather, it is a matter of background of the two eminent personalities. Plato was writing as the great ethically indoctrinated mathematician while Aristotle was no less immured in moral principles, though with a background of scientific investigation of particular objects and events.

Plato advocated the banishment of poetry or mythology from his ideal society because it dealt with myths and nonbeing in general. As a mathematician, however, he was keen to point out the reality of ideas or idols. While the numerical aspects of individual things were inevitable features of observation, there exist also the more abstract numbers or ideas that could be known but not seen. Ideas of number of things he poetically asserted exist beyond the heavens. Thus Plato brought into Greek thinking a dichotomy or dualism within the space-time manifold of existence. While undoubtedly Plato initiated his dualism on the basis of numbers, he assumed that all things and situations were divisible into immediate presences and ideal models or formulae. Thus there exist the idols of justice, goodness, and all things else. The platonic ideas and bifurcation in general may be summed up as similar to equations or relationships in mathematics. Today we separate persons as statistics, averages, as well as concrete living units.

The psychological method of Greek dualism may be described as the reification of the definition or description of things in aggregates. Platonic ideas are simply categories in substantiation or reification. Currently we refer to colority or hueness, decibels, masses, and so on. As a biologist, Aristotle did not need to feature idealistic problems but could confine his work to the traits of organisms as particularities.

CHAPTER IV

TRAGEDY IN SPIRITISTIC CONVERSION

Following upon the decline of Greece and Rome, an entirely novel type of philosophical and psychological attitudes replaced the Greco-Roman objective and naturalistic way of thinking: The post-Greek culture replaced the current worldly reality with notions of a supersensuous world and one which is still to come. Emphasis upon subjectivity became rife and attitudes concerning events were reduced to spirits and the soul later called mind or consciousness. What had happened philosophically was that the dualism of Plato which had nothing to do with spirits or anything beyond astrophysical existence was transformed into a two world system, the material and the spiritual. Persons too were disunited into (a) soul or mentality, and (b) body. Ideas about tragedy were all centered in the mind or soul of individuals. Propositions about righteousness were couched in terms of consciousness, loyalty, and in general the proper moral behavior of men. Many writers on tragedy analyze the Biblical story of Job as an example of the turning to character instead of objective happening in tragical situations. Thus an invention to teach how individuals should behave in the face of extreme adversity is made into a spiritistic description of tragedy.

In addition to the moralistic aspect, writers on the subject of tragedy have found it easy to turn the essence of tragedy into religious channels. The supernatural world encompasses a supreme being who supplies a life eternal to those who believe in him and who live by his grace or condemnation. All tragic circumstances are tied in with the relation of persons to the supreme being. The specific arguments are human suffering, expiation, and atonement, and finally redemption. We append here a few samples of prominent authors who think under the influence of the mind-body tradition.

A. SUBJECTIVISTIC REACTIONS TO DRAMA

The Greek objective culture enjoyed only a short life. As we have indicated above, new intellectual institutions arose to succeed the Greek naturalistic way of thinking. The dualism of Plato was transformed by churchmen into a psycho-physical supernaturalism. The age of faith succeeded the age of reason. Plato's categories became intangible stuff with persons divided into souls and bodies. Souls were spiritual substances outside of space and time and without any of the properties of things and events met with in the ordinary course of events. A mythological universe was developed to include a transcendental monotheistic god, angels, ghosts, demons, and magical powers of various sorts.

The process of creation thus developed was of course the reification of personally accepted values and verbal formulations. Conditions were changed from persons interacting with things and events to egocentric utterances and subjectively perpetrated inexistent entities. Personal inventions were believed to be a new kind of objective existence. Fables, metaphors, and language references were treated as confrontational objects.

So far as concerns the subject of tragedy, the dualism of man led to complete humanism. Tragedy study was reduced to plays with an emphasis upon the activities of invented persons and their many evil interrelations with each other. Tragedy became concerned with declines from affluence to poverty and much was made of misery, suffering, as well as moral and mental decline. The primary tendency was a flight from authentic circumstances and situations toward imaginative conditions.

The shift in attitudes is quite evident in the various definitions of tragedy.

B. HUMANISTIC DEFINITIONS OF TRAGEDY

By way of summarizing the trend of tragedy study, we may repeat that most of the elaborate literature concerning tragedy refers to dramatic presentations or literary tragedy. Moreover, the intellectual framework consists of dualistic or mentalistic philosophy and psychology. Some examples of tragedy definitions are given below.

CHAUCER

Tragedy is to seyn a certeyn storie, As olde bookes maken us memorie, Of hym that stood in great prosperitee, And is yfallen out of heigh degree Into myserie, and endeth wrecchedly.[1]

O'CONNOR

Tragedy is essentially noble reaction to suffering.[2]

An informing symptom of the situation in tragedy studies is observable in the excellent volume of Mandel, who seeks a reliable definition of the term "tragedy." Placing himself squarely in the realm of art, he attempts to improve upon the famous definition of Aristotle and reaches the following statement.

1. Chaucer, G., "Prologue to the Monk's Tale," quoted from Steiner, G., *The Death of Tragedy,* New York, Knopf, 1961, p. 11.
2. O'Connor, W. Van, *Climates of Tragedy,* Baton Rouge, Louisiana State University Press, 1943, p. 46.

MANDEL

A work of art is tragic if it substantiates the following situation: A protagonist who commands our earnest good will is impelled in a given world by a purpose, or undertakes an action, of a certain seriousness and magnitude; and by that very purpose of action, subject to that same given world, necessarily and inevitably meets with grave spiritual or physical suffering.[3]

Admirable as this formulation may be on literary grounds, it is clearly only a guide to the imaginative activities and products of authors or playwrights. Even though Mandel's formulation is really much more than a fixation of a term but also reaches out toward theatrical action, it serves to narrow the field of tragedy to representative situations.

HERDER

Tragedy is the struggle of man with fate. It is a shiksalsfabel.[4]

LUCAS

Tragedy, then, is a representation of human unhappiness which pleases us notwithstanding, by the truth with which it is seen and the fineness with which it is communicated - l'amertume poignant et fortifiante de tout ce qui est voraine.[5]

While G. Steiner despairs about formulating a definition of tragedy ("Any neat, abstract definition would mean nothing"), he does offer a definition in the authentic sense of a description.

---

3. Mandel, O., *A Definition of Tragedy*, New York, New York University Press, 1961, p. 20, 88.
4. Herder, J.F., *Adrastea*, Vol. 2, part 4, in *Sämmtliche Werke*, Vol. 23, Berlin, Werdmann, 1885, p. 355.
5. Lucas, F.L., *Tragedy, Serious Drama in Relation to Aristotle's Poetics*, London, Hogarth Press, 1957, p. 78.

STEINER

Tragic drama tells us that outside and within man is l'autre, the otherness of the world. Call it what you will, a hidden or malevolent God, blind fate, the solicitations of hell, or the brute fury of our animal blood. It waits for us in ambush at the crossroads. It mocks us and destroys us. In certain rare instances, it leads us after destruction to some incomprehensible repose.

From antiquity until the age of Shakespeare and Racine, such accomplishment seemed within the reach of talent. Since then the tragic voice in drama is blurred or still.[6]

HATHORN

A tragedy is a work of literature which has as its chief emphasis the revelation of mystery.[7]

CHU

Tragedy is a work of art shaped by the imagination of a great master.

Tragedy in spite of its origin in religious rites, is preeminently a form of art, and the contemplation of tragedy an aesthetic experience.[8]

KRUTCH

True tragedy may be defined as a dramatic work in which the outward failure of the principal personage is compensated for by the dignity and greatness of his character.[9]

It is quite evident that a job of analysis and separation is in order. Dramas must be separated from other anthropic and nonanthropic events, then a more rationalistic and naturalistic attitude towards tragic events can be adopted.

---

6. Steiner, G., *The Death of Tragedy*, New York, Knopf, 1961, pp. 8-10.
7. Hathorn, R.Y., *Tragedy, Myth and Mystery*, Bloomington, Indiana Univ. Press, 1962, p. 223.
8. Chu, Kwang-Tsien, *The Psychology of Tragedy: A Critical Study of Various Theories of Tragic Pleasure*, Strasbourg, Librarie Universitaire de l'Universite, 1933, pp. 21, 247.
9. Krutch, Joseph Wood, Introduction to *Nine Plays by Eugene O'Neill*, New York, Modern Library, 1932.

PHILOSOPHERS VIEW TRAGEDY

Historically then, tragedy study is primarily the overshadowing of the particulars of plays with the intellectual auras of philosophers, whether professionals or acolytes serving as dramatists, playwrights, critics of literature in general, or specialists of particular plays. In the following examples, we limit ourselves to professional philosophers.

In this second period, the regnant dualism seeps down to the individual and his psychology. The integral organism is bifurcated into a soul and body. The former is the nebulous spirit, really a verbal creation that is given the name "mind," "consciousness," "passions," and similar forms of immaterial soul. In intention, this was presumed to be a deepening way of reaching essentials. In effect, this doubling of the person distorted the acts of protagonists in plays and concealed his acts as he participated in tragic events or situations.

HUME. In his essay called *Of Tragedy,*[10] this philosopher skirts completely tragic events and confines himself to the pleasure which spectators receive from sorrow, terror, anxiety, and other passions (experiences) that are themselves disagreeable and uneasy.

Hume frequently resorts to the view that human nature is such that the mind is stirred by the excitement of the passions and that the irritation produced by dramatic presentations stimulate the pleasure of curiosity as in the case of children.

HEGEL. As a theistic metaphysician, Hegel judged the identity and merits of plays on the basis of an Absolute Idea or Divine Being in which all discord and clashes can be harmonized. Thus the Divine is the proper theme of tragedies. As a religious spiritistic philosopher, Hegel's view of tragedy

10. Hume, D., *Essays,* London, Routledge, n.d.

is replete with notions of subjective passions. It is among them that the disharmony or clashes occur which in the Absolute are harmonized.[11] In general, Hegel traffics with the nonexistent spiritual life, with "inner processes" and not with objective deeds (p. 1168[b]). Plays as dramatic art must correspond to Reason and Spiritual Truth. In the final analysis, it seems clear that Hegel is imposing upon tragic plays and all things else the religious doctrine of wrongdoing, repentance, and reconciliation.

With respect to the frequently posed questions of why people enjoy tragedies, Hegel offers his characteristic verbal solution that the enjoyment arises from the triumph of "Eternal Justice." There is a Reconciliation in the harmonious synthesis of clashings, collisions, and conflicts. The Hegelian system may be regarded as the inevitable stimulus to the development of linguistic philosophy which is aimed at the elimination from writings and thinking of utter verbigeration.

SCHOPENHAUER. This pessimistic thinker, a sufferer from futilistic encounters with unhappy experiences, paints tragedies with somber colors indeed. For Schopenhauer, who believed that the world was only will and idea, agreed with Macbeth that life is but a walking shadow, a poor player that struts and frets his hour upon the stage and is heard no more, wrote of tragedy.

> Tragedy is to be regarded as the summit of poetical art, both on account of the greatness of its effect and the difficulty of its achievement. It is very significant for our whole system, and well worthy of observation, that the end of this highest poetical achievement is the representation of the terrible side of life. The unspeakable pain, the wail of humanity, the triumph of evil, the scornful mastery of chance, and the irretrievable fall of the just and innocent, is here presented to us; and in this lies a significant hint of the nature of the world and of existence.[12]

---

11. Hegel, G.W.F., *Aesthetics*, (T.M. Knox, tr.) Oxford, Clarendon, 1975, vol. 2, pp. 1159, 1168, 1170, 1193, et passim.
12. Schopenhauer, A., *The World as Will and Idea*, R.B. Haldane and J. Kemp (trs.), London, Kegan Paul, 1907, p. 326.

NIETZSCHE. As a writer on tragedy, this pessimistic follower and later repudiator of Schopenhauer shows clearly in his famous book, *The Birth of Tragedy*, a curious confusion of statements connecting Greek with post-Greek spiritistic traditions.[13] Drawing upon his Greek studies, he makes use of the two deities Apollo and Dionysius as a basis for presenting his ideas of the origin and decline of tragedy. As is well known, Nietzsche derives tragic plays from the Dionysian type of living and suffering through music which is engendered when Apollonian light initiates mythology.

Nietzche's thinking is heavily freighted with spiritistic notions. His Dionysian experiences are full of primordial states of mind, crude instincts, elementary feelings, intense passions, brutish acts, and internal intuitions. Apollonian mentality thrives on a higher plane. It is made up of sedate, reflective states, rationality instead of sensuousness, dreaminess and drunkenness instead of the thinker's reality.

Nietzsche makes a great to do about the discarding of the Dionysian ecstasies by Euripides. The latter, he asserts, has killed tragedy because he has listened to the Apollonian promptings of Socrates. Nietzsche declares that the art-work of Greek tragedy was wrecked by the thinking of Socrates and Euripides. Socrates brought about an objective tragedy as opposed to the subjective type.

What did you want, sacrilegious Euripides, when you sought to compel this dying myth to serve you once more? It died under your violent hands-and then you needed a copied, masked myth that, like the ape of Heracles, merely knew how to deck itself out in the ancient pomp. And just as the myth died on you, the genius of music died on you, too. Though with greedy hands you plundered all the gardens of music, you still managed only copied, masked music. And because you had abandoned Dionysius, Apollo abandoned you: rouse all the passions from their resting places and conjure them into your circle, sharpen and whet a sophistical dialectic for

13. Nietzsche, F., *The Birth of Tragedy*, Out of the Spirit of Music, W. Kaufmann (tr.), New York, Random House, 1967.

the speeches of your heroes-your heroes, too, have only copied, masked passions and speak only copied, masked speeches.[14]

When Nietzsche practiced the role of a philosopher, he displayed rather violent attitudes of dissatisfaction with the culture of his time and place, calling for a transvaluation of the values of Christian civilization and morality. But he did not realize, in the slightest, world events as they actually are.

By contrast with literary critics, philosophers go beyond the structures of plays and the scenes depicted. They search for the meanings or the essential significance of what they see represented. Naturally, they stretch out to the nature or characteristics of the protagonists and the acts they perform with relation to each other. All this within the framework of their special philosophical systems. Philosophers impose upon the plays, they assess their own moral and aesthetic principles. Frequently their ideas and ideals are reminiscent of traditional notions of fate and putative forces and powers which have no counterpart really in the plays or players or people, in general, supernatural entities.

The result is the distortion and improper description of human beings, their development, current behavior, and tragedy itself. For this reason, there are so many different interpretations of theatrical exhibitions.

KALLEN. This philosopher of a more ample period of tragedy study reaches out beyond the narrow confines of literature, though he restricts tragedy to human affairs. He asserts that,

Tragic in its own right only mankind can be, and all else is an image and a symbol merely, not a real life, the peer of man's.[15] p. 195

---

14. Nietzsche, F., Ibid., Sections 10-14.
15. Kallen, H.M., "The Essence of Tragedy", *The International Journal of Ethics*, 1912, 17, 179-203.

Specifically, he believes that valuation makes tragedy.

> Where there are no values, there can be no interests and no tragedy. Ibid. p. 189

Still more specifically, he writes,

> It is the destruction of value that primarily constitutes tragedy. Ibid., p. 195

He continues,

> The right essence of tragedy lies not in the demolition of value merely, but in the destruction of value by value. Ibid., p. 197

Considering that Kallen adopts the humanistic view of tragedy, one cannot object seriously to his view. But on the other hand, in view of his dualistic assumptions of psychology and philosophy, there is still a great insufficiency in his interpretation.

In a similar vein, the philosopher Scheler emphasizes the destruction of values by values. He refers to it as the tragic knot.

> Es gibt einen Fall, wo unsere Bedingung, dass ein Widerstreit zwischen Tragern hoher positiver Werte stattfindet und in ihm einer der Trager zugrunde geht, bis zur aussersten Grenze erfullt ist. Das ist dann der Fall, wenn die Wertetrager gar nicht verschiedene Ereignisse, Dinge, Personen sind.[16]

KAUFMANN. Although this philosopher, who is keenly interested in tragic events, writes at a considerably later day, he returns vigorously and effectively to problems of literary tragedy. As the following quotation indicates, he elaborates

16. Scheler, M., "Zum Phänomen Des Tragischen," in *Abhandlungen Und Aufsätze,* (I), Leipzig, Weissen Bucher, 1915, p. 293.

well his interpretation which takes account of the late developments in conventional views of philosophy and psychology. Kaufmann's statement may be regarded as an adequate summary of the entire tradition of literary criticism.

> Tragedy is (1) a form of literature that (2) presents a symbolic action as performed by actors and (3) moves into the center immense human suffering, (4) in such a way that it brings to our minds our own forgotten and repressed sorrows as well as those of our kin and humanity (5) releasing us with some sense (a) that suffering is universal-not a mere accident of our experience, (b) that courage and endurance in suffering or nobility in despair are admirable-not ridiculous-and usually also (c) that fates worse than our own can be experienced as exhilarating. (6) In length, performances range from a little under two hours to about four, and the experience is highly concentrated.[17]

NATURALISTIC TRAGEDY FORMULATED

It appears a necessary conclusion to this chapter and its several sections that it is advisable to move toward a more naturalistic treatment of tragedy in all its forms. In this connection it is appropriate to suggest a rational and naturalistic definition (description) of tragedy.

Tragic events are occurrences, in pristine nature and in human circumstances that are occasionally mild but usually intense, momentous, excessive, and frequently pregnant with grave consequences. Owing to the accident that the name of tragic events is historically coupled with literary sources, the continuity of events has been occluded and therefore unrecognized.

The precise hypothesis adopted in this essay is that tragedy comprises situations in which significant potentialities that have been developed are destroyed or lost in the process of event changes, instead of attaining a complete actuality.

---

17. Kaufmann, W., *Tragedy and Philosophy*, Garden City, Doubleday, 1958, p. 85.

CHAPTER V

THE EVENT CONTINUUM

THE CONTINUUM: OCCURRING EVENTS

Although our special current interest is in tragic events, we cannot forego the consideration of the general event continuum in which tragic events, like all other events, occupy unique points. This continuum comprises all events, whether they occur in pristine nature or in the bounds of hominid culture. Thus the event continuum numbers among its components cosmic and telluric happenings along with humanly contrived and construed things and events, such as plays, dramas, and other literary productions.

Why stress the continuum of events? Answer! It is in the interest of a rational and precise assessment of things and events as they are observed. Events in nature as units are interrelated among themselves as indicated by such mathematical formulae as CH_2OH, H_2O, NaCl, $G=kMM'/r^2$, $T_0=273.16$, H_2CO_3, PE = C(k, sf, rf, hi, st, md), and other descriptions. The same must be said of tragedies in the lives of individuals and groups. Any interpretation of events as supernatural or simply arbitrary and autistic also is a natural event, but obviously only as linguistic utterance. Such interpretations are not imitations of observed events although even fables or myths must bear some relation to events and conditions known about. Much of what is presumed to be tragic may not even be pathetic or pathological.

THE NATURALISTIC APPROACH

The event continuum implies a naturalistic attitude toward the study of events of every type. It is proposed that a wider horizon is today available upon which to build more effective philosophical and psychological postulates for investigating the nature and conditions of both tragical and non-tragical events. Today it is possible to regard tragic events, and every other type, as collocations of circumstances that can be observed and interpreted in a scientific or rational manner. Once satisfactory information is attained concerning events in general, valid judgments become available concerning particular tragic events, whether in the natural surroundings or in literary and art products.

Every significant approach to the problems of tragedy as in every other circumstance entails some basic orientation to the ambient world. In brief, some type of philosophy. A rational background of beliefs and assumptions, that is, a naturalistic philosophy entails the view that the "universe" or "reality" consists of events of various sorts. Events include things, movements, actions, interrelated conditions of change with unique origins, evolutions, and devolutions. It is an understandable circumstance that the evolution of human organisms which is a late development of events from the standpoint of the astronomic universe, should lead to an overemphasis of the place of hominids in the total cosmic scheme. However, it is obvious that the event continuum comprises the immense series of coordinate events generally known as Inorganic, Organismic, and Hominid events.

EVENTS AS ELEMENTS OF THE CONTINUUM

To be naturalistic or scientific, descriptions must be analytic. The details of various event types may not be overlooked or neglected. Modern philosophy and psychology when appreciated can produce an important impact upon all questions concerning tragedy, whether in nature or in culture. They can greatly modify the analyses and interpretations formulated about the various tragic situations. For example, when persons are concerned, they are not regarded as transnatural in any sense, but as concrete entities that are fairly well described by the biological sciences of anatomy, physiology, pathology, and evolutionary origin and development, as well as in the humanistic sciences of sociology and cultural anthropology. As we have indicated in the preface to this work, we must turn radically away from any mysterious or mystic internalities, whether called spiritistic or just subjective. Modern naturalistic thinking can also take account of detailed differences between (a) tragedy as constructions made for show, and (b) actual life conditions which the shows or plays are presumed to represent. A satisfactory analysis of events requires a sharp differentiation between (a) general happenings, and (b) imitated spectacles presented in written form or as acted on a stage. We propose to name the two phases of events as nonanthropic and anthropic occurrences.

EVENTS AS FIELDS OR SYSTEMS

Events of every type consist of fields or systems in which a number or series of objects and conditions converge to form a unit of specific happenings. One of the fundamental features of event fields is that they as well as the components or subunits of the fields are in constant motion or change so that variations are invariable and inevitable. Things or circumstances come into being and pass out of existence with resulting modifications leading to newer objects and fields or recurring patterns of previous forms. Conventional views of tragic fields or situations derived mainly from dramatic traditions have it that tragic events consist of a death of a noted person or beloved one, or in general the loss of something of value, or some calamity on sea, air, or land. Now, it is obvious that the literary view of tragedy is one sided and blocks the appreciation of the basic traits of events in general, as well as those of tragic situations.

EVENTS: ESSENTIALLY CHANGES

The adage that there is nothing constant but change cannot better be manifested than in tragic situations. Change, of course, is the invariable and constant feature of all happenings. Changes are roughly categorized by the touchstone of (a) magnitude (normal shifts, immensity of shifts); (b) situation (whether anthropic or inorganic systems); (c) temporality (seasonal intervals of occurrence); (d) radiational or electromagnetic rate and magnitude of change or charge; and finally, (g) relational changes (type and manner of association of components in a system, reaction of particles in atoms), and general chemical reactions as compared with molecular and compound or gravitational systems.

TRAGEDY PRIMARILY DISTURBANCE OF EQUILIBRIUM

Tragedy is a situation in which the ordinary equilibrium of components in a system or field are disturbed excessively. Equilibrium is primarily a matter of order and order is simply a matter of status, how a thing or event is organized. A biological cell as a thing or event functions as an orderly system. However, the components of the cell may become deranged as cancerous. In inorganic things, disordered systems may approach deficiency of function and attain a measure of entropy. In organismic systems or fields, one may quote the well known circumstance of well and ill being, and the extreme case of neoplasms as in cancerous situations. In general, change of equilibrium or order marks a variance in identity of thing or event. See Gibbs on Equilibrium in physics.*

TRAGEDY STUDY AND HOMINID EVOLUTION

So far as concerns human tragedy, the important circumstances loom that through a very long series of modifications, transformations, and evolutions, mankind appeared and evolved to the point of looking back, as effectively as possible, to the entire evolutional process, and formulating descriptions and interpretations about it, and even to practice inductive inferences about the further occurrence of changes. The study of events including those called tragical is simply the end result of a multiplicity of events which can be described as the evolution of organisms from an inorganic matrix to scholars curious about the origin and development of the continuum. (See Fig. 5-1.)

THE NATURALISTIC IMPACT ON TRAGEDY STUDY

With the burgeoning of modern civilization, many varying attitudes toward tragedy problems have emerged. However, not all the current views have profited from the increase of knowledge and the advancement of the naturalistic outlook upon things and events.

For the most part, tragedy study in the current scene exhibits a palpable dualistic atmosphere. On one hand, there is a great emphasis of interest in the literary aspects of tragedy plus a faint tradition of philosophic analysis, all influenced by the overwhelming aura of phenomenology, spirituality, and psychic attitudes. On the other hand, there has grown up the

*Wheeler, L.P., *Josiah Willard Gibbs: The history of a great mind*, New Haven, Yale University Press, 1951.

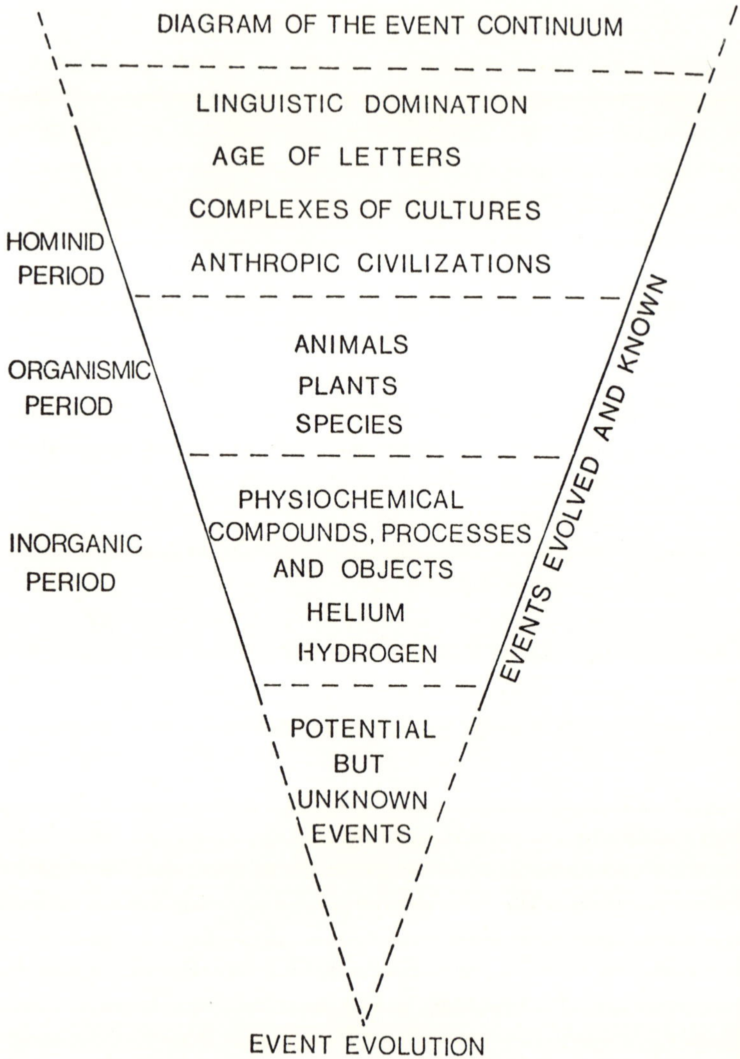
DIAGRAM OF THE EVENT CONTINUUM
LINGUISTIC DOMINATION
AGE OF LETTERS
COMPLEXES OF CULTURES
ANTHROPIC CIVILIZATIONS
HOMINID PERIOD
ANIMALS
PLANTS
SPECIES
ORGANISMIC PERIOD
PHYSIOCHEMICAL COMPOUNDS, PROCESSES AND OBJECTS
HELIUM
HYDROGEN
INORGANIC PERIOD
EVENTS EVOLVED AND KNOWN
POTENTIAL BUT UNKNOWN EVENTS
EVENT EVOLUTION

Fig. 5-1

From a naturalistic standpoint, there appears to be an exaggeration of the dramatic tragedy aspects with a corresponding neglect of tragical situations in both nature and culture. The result is a paucity of appreciation of the nature of drama theories. For example, play production may be regarded as neutralized, as the term "show biz" indicates. In the multifaceted world of play production, play attendance is a specialized and unique feature of living especially in populated centers. Plays as works of art have given place to economic and commercial enterprises. What are called tragedies may not bear the properties of tragedies at all. Certainly, dramas are uninfluenced by intellectual and philosophical considerations. The entertainment motive may dominate the entire process and leave untouched educational and cultural advancement. Basically, of course, there remains a continuity with the spiritistic trends of popular thinking and believing.

The cultivation of the naturalistic method not only assumes the continuity of all events, but also demands taking account of their variations. For example, hominid or anthropic events are treated differently from nonanthropic events.

EVENTS: ANTHROPIC AND NONANTHROPIC

NONANTHROPIC EVENTS. Events of this class are those in which changes and transformations are of weighty dimensions. Obvious examples are great tidal waves, volcanic eruptions, earthquakes, droughts, floods, and whatever losses and destructions are initiated. Such event fields contrast with those in which mild or calm changes occur among the interacting components of total fields. Now despite the fact that persons may be components of the fields, they are natural events and potential factors for the application of some arbitrary term, even that of "tragedy." No autistic term, however, should be applied to them such that some creator, force, or power has intervened to bring about the convulsion or unusual condition.

Since there are no human elements in the nonanthropic fields, the term "tragedy" is not to be applied to events as though it were the name for a quality or property of some thing or field. Names and attitudes toward events of nature consist of descriptive reactions or constructive behavior and products developed concerning events on the basis of their intensity, severity, or quantitative transformation.

ANTHROPIC EVENTS. The characteristic feature of anthropic events is that human individuals and their circumstances are prime factors. The change, loss, decline, or destruction may be that of a hero, or special person, or object of value. Literary tragedies center about such fields. Though different, the anthropic and nonanthropic classes of event fields form a dense continuum. A proper analysis convinces that both classes are objective and naturalistic events. However, the fact that anthropic events entail psychological problems suggests only that psychology itself should be regarded as a definite objective and naturalistic discipline.[1] The accompanying diagram, Fig. 5.2, may help to clarify the relationships between different event fields.

SCHEMA OF EVENT TYPES AND RELATIONS

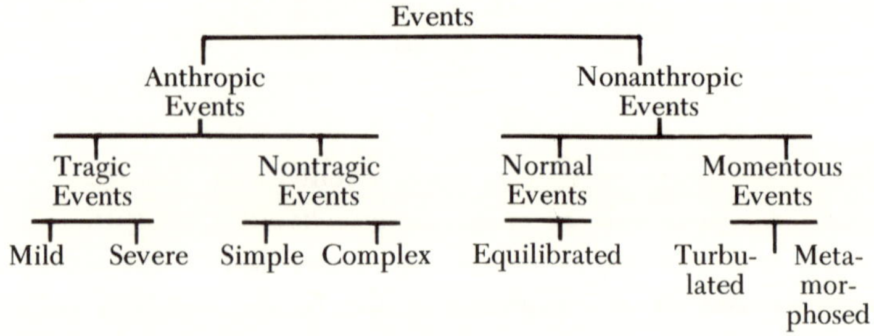

Fig. 5.2.

1. See Chapter VIII.

Granting that tragic events are a particular subclass of natural happenings, their range of instances covers a wide domain indeed. Variations in the subclass members are functions of specific changes in things and their conditions. Accordingly, tragic events comprise (1) nonanthropic events, (2) such anthropic events as the destruction and loss of persons or their possessions in various crises, and (3) the work and products of playwrights who propose to present depictions of human tragedies.

Since tragic events involve magnitudes, relativity, and seriousness, they always admit of some sort of ordering such that tragic events accumulate at the upper extreme of the categorization. A suggestion for such an arrangement may be represented as in Fig. 5.3.

SCHEMATIC DIAGRAM OF POINTS ON THE EVENT CONTINUUM

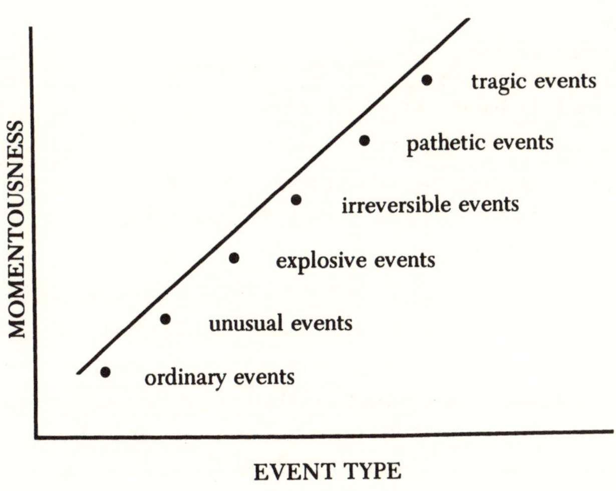

Fig. 5.3.

It will be noticed that the differing interrelated steps vary with the specific type of situation current at any particular time. Also, there are degrees of each category or condition. Ordinary events are more or less ordinary. Similarly, tragedy is a more or less momentous situation. For our present purposes, however, the greatest differences exist between Anthropic and Nonanthropic situations.

EXAMPLES OF NONANTHROPIC TRAGEDIES. Owing to the fact that the study of tragedy has been so strongly influenced by literary scholarship, the death of a hero or other prominent person has come to be a primary example of tragic events. However, from the standpoint of tragedy as natural events, death is only one kind of loss or detriment of value. We have already indicated that the great range of tragic events includes many instances of calamitous transformations, as mentioned above and repeated in the following examples.

Extreme weather conditions
Tidal waves
Hurricanes
Crop failure
Severe erosions
Volcanic actions and eruptions

The list is very long and the effects upon observers very striking and intense in their occurrence and results.

EXAMPLES OF ANTHROPIC TRAGEDIES. Interest in tragic events must carry over to many sorts of deprivation or disappearance of valuable things or qualities, no matter where or when they occur. Since tragedy study must include anthropic situations, they cannot be undervalued. Accordingly, a list of this type of tragic events will include the following.

Human frustrations
Unfulfilled ambitions
Curtailment of personal development
Deaths in certain situations

It is not unreasonable to count as supreme tragedy that hominids have been so retarded in development and general evolution that they have not been able to outlive their crude zoological nature so as to live in harmony and progressive growth in any other way than the primitive jungles in which persons live actually in small or large communities. Required here is the observation that the human species possesses the supreme capacity to develop technological worlds of the greatest moment. One might declare that this skewed development is one of the great tragedies of human existence.

INVERSE OR NEGATIVE TRAGEDY

When tragedy is studied from a naturalistic and scientific viewpoint, one meets with situations that are distinctly inversive. That is the case when there are striking changes or devastation, but no prior concentration or build up of potentialities whose loss would be assessed as disastrous or calamitous. Again there is inverse tragedy when what is changed or destroyed lacks value or significance.

Examples of inverse tragedy are to be cited in every type of event or situation. In political situations, there are many tragic promotions and elections of persons of inferior quality to high office by the defeat of better candidates. Also, in academic circles, it often occurs that the inferior candidate is preferred over a much better scholar. Among army officers (Cassius), is the accusation of selling "offices for gold to undeservers."[2]

Inverse or negative tragedies must be regarded as authentic events, but only in pristine situations. In literary situations, what is called tragedy is neutral, that is, it is out of the range of authentic tragedy altogether.

2. Shakespeare, W., *Julius Caesar,* IV: 3, 11-12.

POTENTIALITY AND ACTUALITY OF EVENTS

Of great importance for the present essay, as well as for scientific study in general, is the clarification of the potential and actual phases of the event continuum. Potentiality is in general terms the evolution of structures and functions of an object or person, of traits, characteristics, and properties, but with the lack of a convergence with other components for the actualization of another specific or unique event field. A commonplace example is the presence of the mixture in the cylinder of an internal combustion engine before the spark that ignites it. Another everyday example is the various knowledges and skills of the doctor, lawyer, engineer, or teacher before the arrival of a patient, client, or students.

All the variables of a field must be conjoined for a change to take place of a succeeding event field. Potentiality is a circumstance of prior actualization which may never participate in any further actuality unless coupled with other potential variables. When any total system of variables converge, that signalizes another event, an explosion, combustion, an effect, in general, a new item in the event continuum.

CHAPTER VI

TRUNCATED POTENTIALITY HYPOTHESIS ILLUSTRATED

On page 36, we have indicated what we regard as a naturalistic definition or description of tragic events. It was intended to indicate the necessity to improve upon the previously formulated descriptions, which were regarded as insufficient or entirely inept.

Tragic events cannot be limited to such simplified situations as painfulness, even in excessive form, as suffering, or as the death of a hero, though such events may appear as component factors in tragic situations. No, we require a more significant interpretation. We propose that tragic situations consist of truncated actuality, momentousness, radical changes, in brief, inordinate occurrences. That is what binds together personal, human, and cosmic happenings in naturalistic similarity. Tragedy is impedence of a dynamic and growing series of events; it is complexity; it is gross and momentous truncation of previously ongoing happenings; it is a radical break in the continuity of event systems.

In this chapter, we collect some illustrations of situations which may be taken as tests of the naturalistic hypothesis. When the tests are favorable, the illustrations serve as confirming evidence. The case studies are drawn from two sources. A, from literary works and B, from actual living conditions. In the latter case, some differentiation is indicated between milder and more severe circumstances.

A

ILLUSTRATIONS OF TRAGIC EVENTS FROM LITERATURE

Although tragic dramas may not comport well with tragic events as they actually occur, still they offer suggestive materials to illustrate the truncation of potentiality in tragic situations. The choice of cases from dramatic representations or literature is random sampling.

IBSEN: LITTLE EYOLF

In this play, Ibsen describes a situation which clearly indicates that the tragic element concerns the loss or cutting off of real or imagined potentialities, as is indicated in the following quotation.

> I will try to perfect all the rich possibilities that are dawning in his childish soul. I will foster all the noble germs in his nature - make them blossom and bear fruit. And I will do more than that! I will help him to bring his desires into harmony with what lies attainable before him. That is just what at present they are not. All his longings are for things that must remain unattainable to him all his life long. But I will create a conscious happiness in his mind.[1]

SOPHOCLES: OEDIPUS REX

As a first example from the Greek theatre, we choose the invention of Oedipus Rex. In our search for tragic elements in this work of Sophocles, we follow the essential plot or scenario of the great and acclaimed hero who drops into the bottom of the lowest depths, carrying a loathsome burden of guilt, blinded, and exiled to wander widely.

---

1. Ibsen, H., *Little Eyolf*, Archer, W. (tr.), Chicago, Stone and Kimball, 1894, p. 42.

As to the exalted status of the King, we note that the priest in the opening of the play calls him the first and noblest of men, the one-time savior of the city of Thebes, the only one capable of repeatedly performing great deeds of political and military salvation.

In the end, however, Oedipus has been condemned and castigated to the lowest rung of the world of horror and infamy. Not that Oedipus lacks admiration, since his honesty and general abhorrence of his own guilt have been noticed and posted to his moralistic credit. Though modern law traditions declare that ignorance is no excuse or exculpatory plea, it is still true in the domain of human frailty that to be unaware of one's transgressions is to be innocent of malice or wrong intent.

The myth of Oedipus, without doubt, illustrates the circumstance of a grand accumulation of excellent potentialities that have been negated by a series of dire circumstances. Sophocles has supplied vivid evidence of the manner in which all the potential of grandeur and glory have been destroyed. Nothing worse than patricide and incestuous behavior could befall the career of Oedipus.

Although the Oedipus myth bears the marks of a powerful inventor, the materials employed are merely exaggerated themes of possibilities in the experience of those who live in the various human communities.

SOPHOCLES: ANTIGONE

Sophocles employs strong measures to build up the basic qualities of Antigone. He makes of her an ideal personality true to her convictions. She is extremely loyal to her brother in opposition to Creon who has issued a stern warning that the slain brother who is accused of vile transgressions against the State should not be buried, but left to the ravage of animals-dogs and vultures.

So the scene is set for a great dilemma which brings cruel agony to Antigone. On the one hand, there are the conventional institutions invoking dire penalties for treasonable acts, while on the other, there are the impulses of brotherly love which cannot tolerate the unburial of the brother. Antigone has attained to such heights as to constitute tremendous potentialities for proper citizenship and a glorious personal life, but the act of burying Polyneices brings in a situation which intensifies the dilemma and makes way for a striking Greek tragedy.

The situation can be approached in a perfectly naturalistic way. We may rule out the cultural factors present when the play was constructed and performed. We leave out all notions of fate and problems of local morality, and regard the entire situation as an extreme happening, in this case, in the lives of people living or imagined to be living at the time of Sophocles.

As the play is constructed, there are present many components of what have always been regarded as features of tragedy, that is, deep suffering, intense agony, but they do not occlude the basic principle that tragic events consist of the curtailment of potentiality attained in the history of personal development.

> Look, leaders of Thebes,
> I am last of your royal line.
> Look what I suffer, at whose command
> because I respected the right.[2]

JUDGES: JEPHTHAH'S DAUGHTER

The biblical story of Jephthah offers an excellent example of tragical events. The situation can no better be pictured than in the original tale.

---

2. Wyckoff, E., in *The Complete Greek Tragedies*, Chicago, University of Chicago Press, 1954.

And Jephthah vowed a vow unto the Lord, and said, If thou shalt without fail deliver the children of Ammon into mine hands, Then it shall be, that whatsoever cometh forth of the doors of my house to meet me, when I return in peace from the children of Ammon, shall surely be the Lord's, and I will offer it up for a burnt offering.

And Jephthah came to Mizpeh unto his house, and, behold, his daughter came out to meet him with timbrels and with dances: and she was his only child; beside her he had neither son nor daughter. And it came to pass, when he saw her, that he rent his clothes, and said, Alas, my daughter! thou hast brought me very low, and thou art one of them that trouble me: for I have opened my mouth unto the Lord, and I cannot go back.

And she said unto him, My father, if thou hast opened thy mouth unto the Lord, do to me according to that which hath proceeded out of thy mouth; forasmuch as the Lord hath taken vengeance for thee of thine enemies, even of the children of Ammon. And she said unto her father, Let this thing be done for me: let me alone two months, that I may go up and down upon the mountains, and bewail my virginity, I and my fellows.

And he said, Go. And he sent her away for two months: and she went with her companions, and bewailed her virginity upon the mountains. And it came to pass at the end of two months, that she returned to her father, who did with her according to his vow which he had vowed.[3]

The potentialities here are of two types. In one, there is the grand circumstance of a successful defender of his group and community and the prospect of a good life within a happy family, including a dutiful daughter fully equipped with the obedience to the local cultural institutions. In the other, there are the potentialities concentrated in a graceful individual displaying her youthful vigor in music and dancing, all cut off by a thoughtless vow. It is interesting to note the attitude of Jephthah's daughter toward death, which loses its sting in the cultural atmosphere of biblical days. The gravamen of the tragic situation is the death of a virgin in a world where marriage is the utmost fulfillment of a woman's life.

PLATO: PHAEDO: DEATH OF SOCRATES

Although the death of Socrates is universally regarded as a tragedy, this does not conform with the naturalistic view

---

3. Judges 11:30.

concerning tragic events. The conventional view is based on the premise that death in itself is a calamity of tragical magnitude. However, though there is a tragic element in the circumstance of Socrates' demise, namely that so great a thinker and human personality should have all his potentialities cut off, the situation in the large may still be questioned as comprising the primary criteria of tragedy.

The ambiguity in the Socratic situation rests solidly on the fact that Socrates did not regard his death as a momentous incident. He speaks of his age, his ethical duty in welcoming punishment as the jury's verdict. Also, as Socrates points out, he could easily have avoided drinking the hemlock by escaping from Athens. The Socratic situation minimizes both death and the destruction of potentiality.

The Socratic example brings forth the duplication of levels in tragic situations. On the one hand, there is the popular level in which the term "tragedy" is allotted to events that may lack momentousness in whole or part, and may be only the outcome of a personal loss. This type of situation is paralleled by the more technical analysis in which principles are involved, that is, problems concerning the nature of tragedy as events in both anthropic and nonanthropic domains.

SHAKESPEARE: CORDELIA

No better literary source of examples of tragical events need be sought than in the plays of Shakespeare, though one may be obliged to dissect out from a mass of disastrous and pitiful happenings. *King Lear*, as a play, amply illustrates this circumstance.

The play universally regarded as a deep and moving tragedy is centered about the misfortunes of an old, foolish, mad monarch engaged in the nonsensical process of dividing an immense kingdom among his three daughters on the basis of how much they love him.

King Lear is a long, complex drama replete with horrible and pitiful incidents which provide rich fare for audiences. But we may think of it as including also an exceedingly prominent situation centered about the youngest daughter Cordelia whose personal qualities comprise a multiplicity of potentialities for a truly human and royal existence.

Shakespeare builds Cordelia up tremendously by comparing her with her dastardly sisters. An almost impossible combination of loyalty, truthfulness, humility, and courage. A person who even in her speech was soft, gentle, and low. An ideal subject to be cast down and subjected to a horrible, murderous death.

It is in order here to reproduce the scene in which Cordelia first enters upon her ordeal. After Goneril and Regan deliver their hypocritical protestations of love, King Lear turns to Cordelia, who says,

> I cannot heave my heart into my mouth. I love your Majesty according to my bond; no more nor less.... You have begot me, bred me, lov'd me: I return those duties back as are right fit; Obey you, love you, and most honour you. Why have my sisters husbands, if they say they love you all? Haply, when I shall wed, that lord whose hand must take my plight shall carry half my love with him, half my care and duty. Sure, I shall never marry like my sisters to love my father all.[4]

The extraction of the Cordelia episode from an extended series of anthropic events requires no apology, since it is clearly evident that Shakespeare has produced a play containing the truncation of great potentiality. It is specific details which provide the substance of tragical events.

SHAKESPEARE: ROMEO AND JULIET

From this play can be extracted a representation of events which qualify well as intensely tragic. The love of Romeo and Juliet set beside the circumstance of the warring

4. Shakespeare, W., *The Tragedy of King Lear,* I:1, 93-95, 98-106.

factions of the Montagues and Capulets has been elevated to a high pitch of potentiality for a good and beautiful life together. Says Juliet,

My bounty is as boundless as the sea,
My love as deep; the more I give to thee,
The more I have, for both are infinite.[5]

A life of affection and attraction stronger than the threats of death and dying. "Shall I be married tomorrow morning. (To Paris) No, no: this (her dagger) shall forbid it."[6] Moreover, as the author has wrought a love so deep and dear, it required potent sets of circumstances to cut it off and destroy it. First, the family circumstances plus the compulsion to marry with Paris, and then such unavoidable accidents of strayed and undelivered messages.

Not all the bloody perversities nor the many by-plays which Shakespeare thought would be of interest and amusement to his audience can cover over the nugget of tragedy which qualifies the play as bearing a truly tragical component.

SHAKESPEARE: MACBETH

In the play by this name, Shakespeare offers us not merely the rise and fall of a person, but also a fine example of a clear cut tragic situation. Of course, his protagonists are mainly Macbeth and Lady Macbeth. Together they act in such a way as to reduce an excellent human and social situation to a "stormy, sinister, and chaotic" condition with horrible consequences. Though Macbeth is held in low esteem as one of the most flawed of Shakespeare's characters, he is, in the play before his downfall, a man of courage, brave, skilled

5. Shakespeare, W., *Romeo and Juliet,* II:2, 133-135.
6. Shakespeare, W., *Romeo and Juliet,* IV:3, 22-23.

in his profession, and endowed with imaginative abilities. A person who would not play false.

Lady Macbeth, however, appears to have had a not too salutary influence upon her husband. She was in great part responsible for the joint evil behavior and indescribably bloody deeds.

As the play indicates, the Macbeth situation was a rosy one. Macbeth was a highly favored one. Thane of Glamis and Cawdor with the prospect of further advancement. All this was thrown down with one monstrous misstep- a temptation to entertain an indecent ambition.

The depths Macbeth descended to are well indicated when he was told the Queen had died.

She should have died hereafter; There would have been a time for such a word. Tomorrow, and tomorrow, and tomorrow creeps in this petty pace from day to day to the last syllable of recorded time; And all our yesterdays have lighted fools the way to dusty death. Out, out brief candle! Life's but a walking shadow, a poor player that struts and frets his hour upon the stage and then is heard no more. It is a tale told by an idiot, full of sound and fury, signifying nothing.[7]

SHAKESPEARE: CORIOLANUS

In this complex and lengthy politically centered play, Shakespeare has managed to provide several illustrations of curtailed potentiality.

The outstanding item is, of course, the great military powers and successes of Caius Marcius at Corioli which eventuated in his nomination as Council. But all his fine Roman qualities and patent accomplishments even as savior of Rome are cataclysmically brought to nothing, and Coriolanus is driven from Rome, "an enemy to the people and his country."[8]

---

7. Shakespeare, W., *Macbeth,* V:6, 17-28.
8. Shakespeare, W., *Coriolanus,* III:3, 119.

Another, if not so definite an illustration is the Shakespearean build-up of Caius Marcius to the strong independent personality, a proud patrician who yet melts into compliance and persuasion despite his vow of vengeance for his despisal and banishment from his beloved Rome.

A third example is that of Coriolanus, the grand and powerful warrior, still to be thought of as a dangerous man to be put to death as an insolent villain, a despised traitor.

As a reinforcement of the interpretation of the tragic aspects of Shakespeare's Coriolanus, we notice that at the close of the play, Affidius, who in his rage ordered the killing of Coriolanus, still asserts the greatness of his erstwhile friend and enemy.

> My rage is gone, And I am struck with sorrow. Take him up. Help, three o' th' chiefest soldiers; I'll be one. Beat thou the drum, that it speak mournfully; Trail your steel pikes. Though in this city he Hath widowed and unchilded many a one, Which to this hour bewail the injury, Yet he shall have a noble memory. Assist.[9]

SHAKESPEARE: OTHELLO

The tragical features of this play center about the relationship of two highly placed persons, Othello and Desdemona. The marriage of the couple appeared a decidedly happy one, Othello a devoted lover and husband, and Desdemona, a loyal and virtuous wife. However, through the machinations of an ingenious and unscrupulous villain, Iago, they were plunged into a catastrophic situation ending in the murder of Desdemona and the suicide of Othello.

The magnitude of the tragedy is measurable by the destruction of the immense potentialities present for an exalted life of service to the state of Venice and an excellent companionship with Desdemona.

---

9. Shakespeare, W., *Coriolanus,* V:6, 147-155.

Othello was a person of high achievement and admiration. He was depicted as

> the noble Moor whom our full Senate call all in all sufficient . . . the nature whom passion could not shake, whose solid virtue the shot of accident nor dart of chance could neither graze nor pierce.[10]

The quality of the domestic relationship with Desdemona is mirrored in Othello's declaration,

> My soul hath her content so absolute that not another comfort like to this succeeds in unknown fate . . . I cannot speak enough of this content.[11]

For those who watch closely the event continuum, take note of similar tragedies in which persons of quality may be influenced by innocent or guilty plotters to mislead and destroy them. In vernacular speech, such events are described as brain washing.

> O thou Othello, that wast once so good, Fall'n in the practice of a cursed slave.[12]

SHAKESPEARE: KING RICHARD III.

In this play, Shakespeare has not offered a typical pattern of tragic proportions in which the protagonist is deprived of peerless potentiality by unusual circumstances. But as a model showing the nature and significance of potentialities, he has supplied material support for the hypothesis we are proposing.

At the very opening of the play, Richard bewails the lack of traits requisite for the life of royal persons. The kind of potentiality that marks tragedy deliberately turns to alternative experiences.

---

10. Shakespeare, W., *Othello,* IV: 1, 275-279.
11. Shakespeare, W., *Othello,* II: 1, 193-195; 198.
12. Shakespeare, W., *Othello,* V: 2, 291.

> I that am rudely stamped and want love's majesty to strut before a wanton ambling nymph— I— that am curtail'd of this fair proportion, cheated of feature by dissembling nature, deform'd, unfinish'd, sent before my time into this breathing world scarce half made up, and that so lamely and unfashionable that dogs bark at me as I halt by them— Why, I, in this weak piping time of peace have no delight to pass away the time . . . And therefore, since I cannot prove a lover to entertain these fair well-spoken days, I am determined to prove a villain and hate the idle pleasures of these days.[13]

GOETHE: MARGARETE

So vigorous are presented the pangs and sufferings of Goethe's Margarete as examples of deep tragedy that they serve to differentiate between the tragedy of dramas and that of analytic descriptions. True enough, the sufferings that Goethe heaped upon Margarete in his book, the supreme *Faust*, are universally regarded as bearing the tragic appellation. But it must not be overlooked that the term "tragic" is part of the vocabulary of popular description and personal perspective as well as that of dramatic criticism and the analysis of tragic events.

From a scientific standpoint, there are lacking entirely the traits that intrinsically deserve the classification of tragic happenings. There is no presumption of a build up of traits of value beyond the everyday conditions of lovers plus the temptations and the yieldings that are so commonplace. Nothing in this judgment should be regarded as reflecting upon the author and his great work. It is to be remembered that *Faust* is a literary construction and not a scientific treatise.

Goethe's Margarete does not so much serve as a direct illustration of tragedy but rather as a fine example of the difference between authentic tragedy and the imitations invented by playwrights and the writers of literary works.

13. Shakespeare, W., *King Richard III*, I:1, 16-31.

B

ILLUSTRATIONS OF TRAGIC EVENTS IN GENERAL HUMAN EXPERIENCE

Because of greater familiarity, illustrations from actual living conditions may be superior to the examples provided by dramatic productions. In the former, definite potentialities are easily observed to be distorted or destroyed. Also, tragedies in actual experience cover a vast spectrum of situations. However, in the present context only a few categories of tragic events can be pointed out.

DEATH OF A BRILLIANT STUDENT. A very definite example of a tragic situation is that of a brilliant student who has throughout his career been building up potentialities that are very much admired and very much valued. Success in learning and advancement is evident and documented by the records of colleges and universities. All this potentiality is tragically annihilated by some accident, say the crashing of an airplane or car, or the derailing of a train which has suddenly and forever cut off the career of the individual as a prospective graduate and teacher. In this situation as in most others, it makes no difference what specific agency operates to destroy the potentiality that has been so carefully and perhaps painfully built up.

MISGUIDED SCIENTISTS. An extremely critical tragical event concerns scientists who have built up a sizeable potentiality from discoveries, teaching, popular acclaim, and scientific recognition by huge prizes for known capacities and performances, but allow early training to influence their interpretations of their findings and scientific discipline.

The history and practice of science offer examples in multitudes of this category of tragical happening. For example, there is the astounding statement of Planck, who had added considerably to the advancement of his scientific specialty, but who ended up with the cry, "Back to God." Then there are the duplex biologists who believe in two forms of knowledge, one of which is intuition, remote from the work of observation, experimentation, and the logic of science, while the other is drawn from following the rules of scientific labor.

STRICKEN IDEAL FAMILY. A poignant tragical situation is that in which the development of a growing family is shattered. In the most intensely tragic case, the family has all the promise of a happy, devoted, and progressive existence. But then an unexpected blow strikes one or more of the members which wipes out all the potentialities until then existing in the promising group. Less poignant tragedies of similar order are marked by a lesser concentration of potentialities. In all instances are present a great number of agencies which disrupt the equilibrium and stability of ongoing events. They may be such factors as floods, fires, diseases, or social and economic circumstances.

GROUP TRAGEDY. In the event continuum, there are tragedies affecting groups as well as only single individuals. It is a most grievous tragedy that the entire human race of Homo Sapiens should display so skewed a development so that some individuals are able to perform supreme feats such as produce great works, like art, inventions of marvellous tools, machines, instruments, and feats like exploring the moon, and still not be able to live with others in peace, harmony, and interethnic cooperation.

SUPPRESSED ORIGINALITY. A unique category of tragic events is localized in situations in which qualities of originality in various domains like thinking, drawing, painting, or industrial and engineering situations are suppressed. One of the most critical examples is alleged to be the public educational or school systems in which all participants are presumed to be alike in capacity and needs. What is alleged to be the result is the suppression of originality and individuality. Tragedies of this category affect individuals and groups alike.

CHAPTER VII

SEMANTIC COMPLICATIONS IN TRAGEDY STUDY

Semantic problems emerge and make trouble in all phases of human existence. It hardly could be otherwise since mankind as cultural organisms is invariably linguistic, while speech and symbolization are clearly subject to uncertainties, ambivalence, and confusion. As it happens too, intercommunications about events and situations are probably more subject to misunderstandings than is the case in other intellectual situations. For the most part, the terms used and the discussions entered into concerning tragedy are faulty on account of the following three circumstances: (a) they are set in unacceptable philosophical and psychological frameworks; (b) they are localized in everyday vocabularies; and (c) they are restricted to drama and staged performances.

SEMANTIC DIFFICULTIES CONCERNING TRAGEDY

So important is it to clarify and correct the semantic difficulties of tragedy study in an attempt to avoid uncritical and irresponsible speech or inexact technical descriptions that we must give the above three circumstances our analytic consideration.

(A) INADEQUATE PHILOSOPHICAL AND PSYCHOLOGICAL PREMISES. The inevitable philosophical and psychological postulates to be found in the conventional literature on tragedy reveal both (1) unacceptable spiritistic factors which mar the intellectual vision, and (2) consequent interpretations about events in general, the nature of man, and the circumstances which make for weal and woe. In consequence, the language employed in the literature of tragedy is replete with theological terms referring to a deity, fate, goodness of god, and so on.

(B) POPULAR EXPRESSIONS. The lack of a sound basis for speech and language leaves open the use of the term "tragedy" for every and any kind of reference without due regard to analytical questions concerning events and their relative qualities.

What is the proper referent for the term "tragedy"? In view of the grand tradition of drama study, it is convenient to separate out the ambiguous or doubtful answers. Tragedy is not just pain, suffering, the death of a hero, but something more significant, as we have been pointing out. Tragedy is the impedance of potentiality, the cutting off of the potentialities that have been developing up to the breaking point.

(C) THE THEATRICAL DILEMMA. Among the outstanding semantic difficulties in tragedy contexts is, of course, the institutionalization of the term "tragedy" as the name for human occurrences as depicted in dramatic literature. That means that the term has taken on referential functions inimical to the widening of the intellectual horizon to encompass other events that are independent of persons altogether. Owing to the aura of the familiar literary tradition, writers overlook the fact that authors of plays derive, though at long range, the qualities and effects they imitate from the qualities of events, that only include but are not based on human affairs. To limit the term "tragic" to anthropic events is to embrace a philosophical identification of speech with the things spoken of.

SEMANTICS IN PROFILE

As a precautionary measure for dealing with semantic problems, it is expedient to make a brief excursion into the semantic phase of linguistics. Scientific linguistics points the way to the fact that language utterances and their literary fixations are always referential reactions to referents. Speech or language consists then of a field or system in which a speaker or writer refers someone to some object or situation as referent.

Upon analyzing linguistic fields which vary radically, we find the following situations.

1) References are made to proximate existent referents as in the simple field of saying, "Please pass the salt."

2) References are made to distal existent referents as in "Circumstances in Latin America look desperate."

3) References are made to nonexistent referents as "Pegasus," "human immortality," "demons," "angels."

4) Variant references to particular existent objects or conditions as in different language systems. Examples: ("der hut," "the hat"), ("mudguard," "fender").

5) Words or terms used vaguely and indiscriminately. No specific referent.

6) Negative language. Action field absent. Objects as potential referents present in plenty, but no references are being made to them.

The accompanying diagram, Fig. 7.1., represents the primary factors in actual speech, writing, and hearing. The essential happenings consist of oral-aural intercommunication, writing, or reading. In technical psychological description, the intercommunication situation consists of a reciprocal field in which a speaker (S) performs a referential reaction, whether an oral utterance or some gestural action with respect to a listener or hearer (S_1) concerning some stimulus object called a referent (R_1). The answer consists of S_1 speaking to S about R_2. In all such events, specific circumstances prevail which facilitate or inhibit proper intercommunicating adjustments.

DIAGRAM OF INTERCOMMUNICATIVE SPEECH

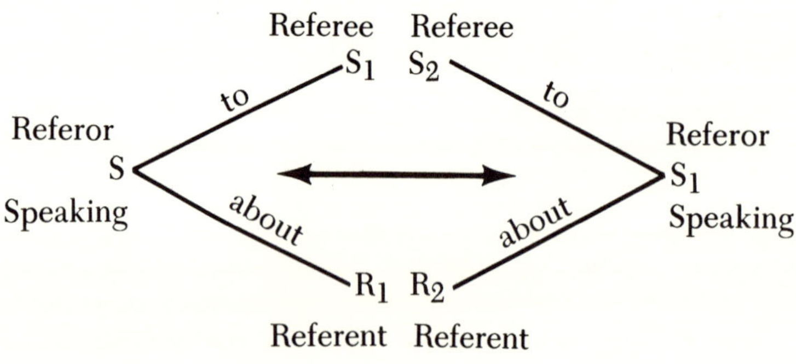

Fig. 7.1.

In view of the particular traits of linguistic fields, it is clear how language can be abused. Words can be transformed into things, metaphors can be taken for concrete realities, behaviors or speaking acts can be turned into objects. All these are misinterpretations and transformations of authentic and serious language fields.

Since human beings are speaking animals, speech behavior fields are extremely common and integrated while the components all exist in their independent states when no speech interbehavior is occurring at some particular time and place. The question arises as to why the term "tragedy" should be limited as a form of reference just because of familiar usage. This is really an anomalous circumstance in view of the flexibility of language fields. So much of linguistic behavior whether speech or text consists of analogy, arbitrariness, and just plain dependence upon various specific conditions. Examples are the fabulous, the hypocritical, "I am very glad to see you," the fairy tales, and white and black lie telling. Why should the term "tragedy" be withheld from serious and momentous happenings in nature?

INFLUENCES OF WORD USAGE

What lends great weight to the semantic problems of any situation is that faulty language can interfere with correct thinking and proper analysis of events. The unwillingness to speak of nonanthropic tragedy prevents the analysis of the magnitude or significance of events and especially the similarities between the condition of anthropic and nonanthropic events. The unsatisfactory outcome of this lack of observation is at least the danger of not doing justice to events and the failure to reach proper descriptions and interpretations of them.

That the event continuum is generally ignored by students of tragic events is at least partially attributed to linguistic conditions. It is the conventional word "tragedy" that tends to conceal the basic traits or characteristics of events. Although at one time the word "tragedy" was used as a reference to songs, it later became closely associated with plays ending calamitously. What became stressed was the human aspect and not the disturbances, gross changes, and the general translocations of things and events. Because of the spiritistic philosophical climate there arose an excessive stress on the soul or mind of organisms or persons, so the continuum of events in which human calamities are only a small part was neglected and forgotten. Events of a tragic type became the exclusive referents of tragedy or tragical happenings. The events that peeped through the play acting were thought of as human problems. As the Oxford English Dictionary indicates, only figuratively does the term "tragedy" refer to serious events in actual living such as dreadful calamities or disasters.

NAMES AND THE NAMING PROCESS

What is a name? This question bobs up strikingly in the context of tragedy study, for example, when it is asserted that inorganic or nonanthropic events are tragic. That sounds odd, mainly because it is seldom or never done. But a strong claim for doing so is the probability that it may be of great help in understanding events in general, including anthropic happenings and even judgments concerning stage performances in dramaturgical study. So important is it to be clear about names and naming that the following answer to the above question is an appropriate one. A name is an arbitrary title, by self or other bestowed, a verbal usage, a construction whether or not fitting some object, event, or nothing at all. But names are not bereft of convenience either for sheer reference or identification or just satisfying convention. To make tragedy an exclusively human thing is to elevate mankind and deny nature.

Cultural or humanistic entities are artificial institutions like all laws, customs, rites, rights, language, and family relationships. The naturalistic attitude toward name problems precludes the influence of the useless abstractions of philosophy, epistemology, and ontology, and asks only if a name, description, or interpretation is derived from events or is autistically appied to something, even a nonexistent object or event.

Many are the procedures for naming things and events. Perhaps the closest to sheerly arbitrary procedures are the naming of offspring by parents. Like all naming procedures, some person or persons do the naming. Parental procedures, however, may not be totally arbitrary when account is taken of the namers concerning their notions, hopes, and family circumstances.

An instructive inorganic naming procedure is available in connection with the naming of the chemical elements. Frequently the aim is to take account of the properties of the elements, or of the credit of the discoverer. The astronomical world offers a fine example. When Herschel discovered Uranus in 1781, he proposed to call it Georgeum Sidus in honor of King George III, but other astronomers wished to honor the discoverer by calling it Herschel, though they finally accepted the name Uranus proposed by the German astronomer Bode. At this point, it is appropriate to suggest once more that the only sure way to describe events is to keep in intimate contact with them and not be misled by words or terms that have become institutionalized and thus capable of stirring up intellectual difficulties.

At this point, it is interesting to note a dim appreciation that practical naming procedures display concerning the event continuum. Plumbers and plumbing material dealers make use of such names as male and female parts for various items.

Also, the computer age has brought about the naming of machine and hardware operations by analogy with human behavior. To computers are ascribed memory, storage and retrieval, thinking, reasoning, and intelligence. Moreover, the general development of technological automation has broken down the linguistic barrier between humanistic things and events and artificiality plus robotism.

CAUTIONARY CONCLUSION

While concluding this chapter, we must add that in no sense are we simply proposing to call an object of nature such as an earthquake a tragic event, especially in the absence of human casualties. On the contrary, our aim is to search for evidence of destruction and dislocation that will eventuate finally in a better understanding of tragic and nontragic events wherever or whenever they occur.

In accordance with the hypothesis of the event continuum, we propose that what is called tragedy in anthropic situations be extended to nonanthropic situations. The significance of the term "tragedy" is a change in the system of factors in any transformation in an event field or system. In general, there is a change or shift in the equilibrium of the field. In nonanthropic fields, the change is a shift from equilibrium to confusion or entropy; later equilibrium is reestablished to be again disturbed or transformed. In anthropic situations, more humanistic terms are available and employed. As we have indicated, the term "tragedy" is universally accepted for what is variously regarded as the ultra disastrous transformation of a humanistic situation.

It is in point here to suggest that the validity of any hypothesis or premise concerning events can be estimated by the touchstone whether a theory or other construction has been derived from similar or analogous events and how well it matches those events. The factor of derivation is extremely important. That signifies the constraint that evidence or presumed evidence is not sought merely to justify some autistic hypothetical formula. There remains, of course, the possibility that inadequate judgments are often available to guard the supposed authenticity of the theory or interpretation, as well as the judgment concerning the independence of the events chosen as the proper evidence for the derived theory.

CHAPTER VIII

PSYCHOLOGICAL ASPECTS OF TRAGIC EVENTS

Anthropic tragedies, though only one of two types of events, count by far as the most popular. This is, of course, explained by the interest of human personalities in the well or ill being of their own kind and the ease with which tragic events can be witnessed and ministered to, as in cultural literature.

Anthropic types of tragical situations obviously involve psychological factors in various forms. Human events comprise particular personalities and the ways they act, in momentous situations and under critical circumstances. Drama critics are constantly concerned with the characters of protagonists in literary tragedies. They make much of hamartia, the fault or flow of character. Accordingly, psychology should have a distinctive place in the study of tragic events.

Furthermore, a scientific approach to tragic events requires a naturalistic treatment of the psychological aspects rather than the traditional discipline that has dominated psychological writings for many centuries.

MODEL OF SCIENTIFIC PSYCHOLOGY

As the name psychology suggests, the discipline now called psychology has developed from the spiritistic matrix of religion and philosophy following the destruction of the Greek and Roman cultures. The entire civilization of western peoples became permeated with the otherworldly aura of the Orient. Truth and reality were to be sought in the hereafter and not in the world of work, conflict, destruction, and of invariable changes. Observation and experimentation concern mainly interrelations of components in fields or systems of events. It was on this basis that tragic events came to be associated exclusively with persons to the exclusions of other sorts of events.

It must be noticed that what is referred to as spiritistic entities consists of nothing more than verbal utterances without regard to the actualities met with in ordinary experience.

A psychological field consists of the interaction of an organism or person with some other person, object, or situation. By virtue of scientific description, the former is spoken of as the response of the organism and the objects interacted with as the stimulus object. Other components of the psychological field consist of auspice conditions plus a medium of interaction commonly referred to as media, as light is a medium for vision and sound is a medium for auditory interactions.

The diagram accompanying Fig. 8.1. may be helpful in the appreciation of the nature of scientific fields, especially a scientific psychological field.

IMPACT OF SCIENTIFIC PSYCHOLOGY ON TRAGEDY STUDY

Since scientific or naturalistic psychology is firmly based on observable fields as units of the event continuum, it can illuminate many problems concerning tragic events. Among the most significant advantages provided by a naturalistic psychology is the naturalizing effect upon philosophical thinking and the provision of valid postulates as bases for analyzing

DIAGRAM OF SCIENTIFIC PSYCHOLOGY EVENTS

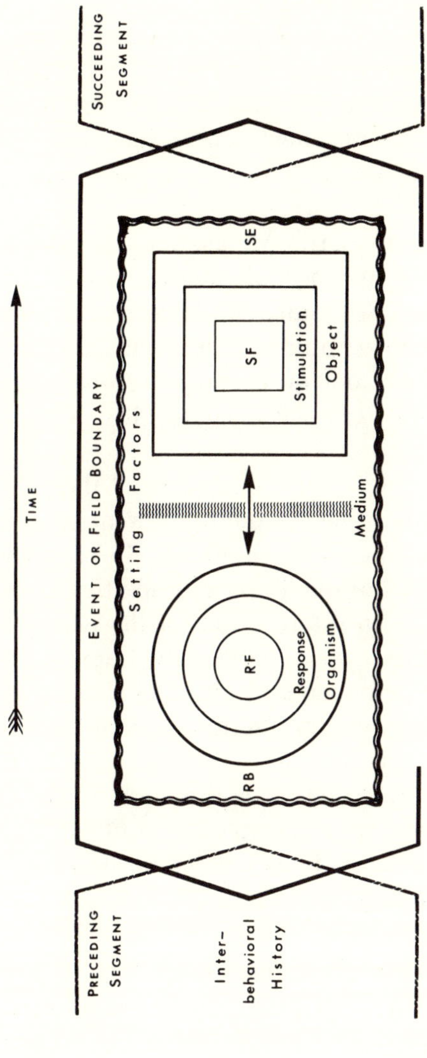

Fig. 8.1. Behavior Segment (or Unit Psychological Event)
RB = Reactional Biography; RF = Response Function;
SE = Stimulus Evolution; SF = Stimulus Function

and interpreting events. Naturalistic psychology thus provides an open highway to rational attitudes with respect to tragedies in all their phases.

A primary consequence is the ready assent to the propositions that anthropic and nonanthropic tragedies are all events, though made up with different components of things and patterns. It is pertinent here to review the differences between the basically inorganic and organic types.

INORGANIC TRAGEDY. An analysis of inorganic tragedies indicates the occurrence of intense changes in the components of systems of cosmic and terrestrial objects, conditions, and relations in complete independence of human beings who may or may not observe the events. We have already pointed to some examples of inorganic tragedies.

ORGANISMIC TRAGEDY. An analysis of the psychological aspects of tragedy brings to the fore the quintessential basis of the anthropic type of tragic events. In each case there is a convergence of the qualities or properties of tragical things or conditions, with the reactions of the participants or spectators to constitute tragic fields. The tragic event then exhibits the basic components of all psychological events, that is an organism involved in a serious situation with more or less enormous occurrences and consequences. In the following paragraph, a brief analysis is presented of the psychological functions viewed from the standpoint of (A) as direct participants in the field, or (B) as a spectator of a contrived or constructed tragic field.

A. *Participant Tragedy.* In this type of tragic field, the individual is the chief protagonist, the sufferer, the victim, the one destroyed, or his behavior is a factor pertinent to his present trouble. He has chosen badly in his decisions and tastes, is now in the wrong or unfavorable trade, profession, marriage, or civil status.

To a great extent, participants in tragic fields are involved with other persons and their behavior. Tragic events may be fraught with every variety of character, misguidance, and errors that make for troubles, difficulties, and losses.

B. Persons as Spectators of Tragedy. Most of the literature on tragedy focuses on tragic events as a thing interacted with. The tragedy may be a natural occurrence or the artifactual presentation of the theatre. In psychological terminology, problems are raised as to the quality of the spectators' reactions. Does he act as though in a very serious situation? What effect does the spectacle have upon him?

SPECIFIC ISSUES IN TRAGEDY STUDY

Students of dramatic tragedies have encountered problems bearing upon historical aspects and upon specific questions concerning the composition of plays and their relevance to striking events in nonliterary situations. Scientific or naturalistic psychology can be of great help in clearing up such problems. Scientific psychology can provide accurate and useful information about significant details of tragic situations. It is convenient to treat such issues under three categories reminiscent of early Greek writings, namely Mimesis, Hamartia, and Catharsis.

MIMESIS. Scientific psychology in any and every circumstance is concerned exclusively with concrete interactions of organisms with any and all of the things and conditions which function as stimulus objects. Accordingly, psychology can throw light on the construction, exhibition, and judgments about tragic situations.

Writers differ about the referent of the Greek term "mimesis." Most translators offer the term "imitation," but although there are many objections,[1] there can be little doubt that in the literary context, the referent should be tragic circumstances of human beings. Consequently, all ghosts, witches, or any other form of deus ex machina should be excluded from the materials of tragic literature.

But for naturalistic psychology, there is a more positive aspect of play writing and that is to keep close to plots that mirror somewhat events that can be observed to happen. Since play writing is construction and creation, rational guide lines are available for order and sense even though the basic motive may be satisfying an audience and increasing one's income.

HAMARTIA. All anthropic tragic events include the qualities or properties of things and conditions in reciprocal interaction with the behavior of persons. Thus many scholars of the history and practice of literary art raise psychological questions though they do not find good answers on the basis of spiritistic psychological premises. Some of the questions concern the character of the protagonists. Hamlet is said to be weak and indecisive, while Othello was strong and practically aggressive. Also, it is held that protagonists frequently do not act according to their "natural" characters. Persons are believed to perform behavior which is out of line with their "native" or habitual development.

Another prominent psychological question concerns those who are not in the play, but react to the plays as spectators. Why, it is asked, do people attend plays and enjoy them when they see upon the stage great destruction, the belittling of persons, and see innocent persons made to suffer. Hardly any play critic fails to consider Aristotle's answer to

1. cf. Kaufmann, W., *Philosophy and Tragedy*, Princeton University Press, 1968.

the effect that to witness the horrors of tragedy is to be purged of pity and fear.

Scientific psychology is unsympathetic to an immediate and single answer. In the first place, it cannot overlook that different persons will react differently to the same horrible presentation; some will be greatly disturbed, while others will find it amusing. A general category of reactions is that of entertainment. Persons attend plays because they are entertained; viewing horrors on the stage is something to do, a break from the experiences of the day. Also, there is entertainment in going to the theatre with some companion.

In an interesting article on Binet,[2] Professor T.H. Wolf has indicated how the famous French psychologist was devoted to the production of horror plays which were presented on the stage of Le Theatre du Grand-Guignol in Paris where the director specialized in plays of horror and terror. Hamartia is sometimes explained as catharsis, but this is based on just another futile attempt to cover a complex situation by a simple single feature. Actually, catharsis itself is a complicated event whose treatment can serve as a touchstone for assaying the value of viewpoints concerning tragic events.

CATHARSIS. Almost every writer on tragedy turns to Aristotle's *Poetica* as a masterly document though many scholars object to his catharsis principle on the grounds that it is too singular as an explanation and too therapeutic. The former criticism is surely a reasonable one, but the objection to catharsis suggests a clash of psychological views. Beneath the surface, the critics stand upon a spiritistic type of psychology as over against the naturalistic view of Aristotle.

Despite Aristotle's minimization of general tragic events, he was clear with respect to his description of the

2. Wolf, T.H., "A New Perspective on Alfred Binet: Dramatist of Le Theatre de L'Horreur," *Psychological Record*, 1982, 32, 397-407.

psychological principles of human behavior. It must be observed that he is concerned with the behavior of persons in tragic situations without the dichotomization of persons into souls and bodies. Organisms for him, whether human or subhuman, are treated as confrontable objects. In this respect, Aristotle may be regarded as an anticipator of modern objective psychology. Naturally, as a biologist of ancient times his views about organismic behavior were quite simple and primitive.

Aristotle's view of tragedy then, as objective as it might be, does not appeal to modern literary critics because of his assertion that the effect of viewing a tragic play is the catharsis of pity and fear. From a modern psychological standpoint, two of the corrections must be made in Aristotle's position, but on other grounds. In the first place, his view must be enlarged to include nonliterary forms of tragedy. Insofar as play tragedy is concerned, a question might be raised whether the tragedy is serious enough to induce any complex affective process, and if the tragedy is momentous, whether there are not other feelings besides pity and fear. We can only guess what Aristotle would have said about nonliterary tragedy. At any rate, we must not expect that a Greek scientist would have information or theories about complicated situations that have developed long after his time.

CHAPTER IX

MULTIVARIATE CONDITIONS INVOLVED IN TRAGIC EVENTS

A naturalistic study of tragedy entails the specification of the circumstances under which tragic events occur. To consider the relevant conditions attending tragic events not only aids in the differentiation of tragedy from other types of events in the continuum of happenings, but also adds to the understanding of scientific observation and analysis. However, such analyses are frankly fraught with considerable difficulties since there are so many peripheral items related to the various tragical fields. Furthermore, specialized experts are necessary to deal with different types of tragic fields, for example, the anthropic and nonanthropic tragedies.

CONDITIONS OF NONANTHROPIC TRAGEDIES. It is clearly evident that the analysis of nonanthropic systems requires the service of the astronomer, physicist, chemist, geologist, seismologist, and other experts familiar with the destructive and calamitious circumstances of cosmic and telluric events. Philosophers and psychologists must resort to such experts for information about the potentialities and actualities of air, water, and land, plus the influences of other planets and stars in the various galaxies. There is here a significant problem of the relationship of potentiality, with respect to the structure and function of the components, which when they converge eventuate into specific and definite effects or events. In view of the enormous range of things and events, the converging components may result in a beautiful object, a successful venture, or a destructive explosion.

In general, of course, account must be taken of the systems comprising the things and events of nature plus the changes that are constantly taking place in them. As an effective criterion, we may assume that the changes taking place in systems are transformations in the equilibrations of the systems. Shiftings are invariably occurring in the components of atoms and molecules with relation to each other or with the ambient conditions. In both cases, there are gradual or sudden modifications, disturbances, alterations, and destructions. In inorganic changes by contrast with anthropic situations, it is the immensity, intensity, and the dimensions of the transformations which are tragic. Mild transformations will result in minor disturbances of equilibrium.

Students interested in nonanthropic tragedies can find much to ponder about in the consideration of the Gibbs phase rule, though the eminent physiochemist was not concerned with possible comparisons with anthropic events. The Gibbs principle of changes in equilibrium, which he treated as freedom of modification, is highly informing as to the composition of substances and the conditions such as temperature and pressure which influence the equilibrium of systems and their components. It is pertinent to present his formula.

$$F = C - P + 2, \text{ or}$$
$$C + 2 = F + P$$

where F = freedom, C = components, and P the number of phases, that is, the solid, liquid, and gas states.

As to suggestions for the proximate and distal conditions or circumstances attending nonanthropic events, resort must be had to treatises on various specialized disciplines such as seismology, thermodynamics, geophysics, and other works on pristine events. There we can learn what is known or inferred about land and mud slides, dust storms, erosions, tidal waves, extreme weather conditions, hurricanes, crop failures, deserts and marshlands, volcanic eruptions, and earthquakes.

For present purposes, it will be sufficient to limit our list of nonanthropic conditions to the representative case of earthquakes. Seismologists report about the subterranean changes centering about the faults and fissures in the earth's crust and the waves of underground rock masses which constantly occur, whether sudden or periodically regular.

The basic value of stressing inorganic changes and transformations is the information they afford as to possible similarities with anthropic system transformations so that in the final analysis, they can contribute to the possibility that inorganic and organic transformations may be regarded as phases of the general event continuum in a naturalistic interpretation of anthropic tragedies.

CONDITIONS OF ANTHROPIC TRAGEDIES. Anthropic events are more intimately familiar to philosophy and psychology, since humanistic tragic situations consist of (a) directly some damage or loss to a person, or (b) indirectly the loss or destruction of some object or circumstance that makes a considerable difference to some person.

An outstanding condition of tragic events relates to the characteristics of the persons involved therein. Consider a situation in which the primary feature of the event is the death of a child. For some parents, the death attains the magnitude of a deep tragedy. For others, the death is simply a normal family event. It may be a family with a number of children, perhaps a primitive one or a member of a relatively unsophisticated group. In a group where infanticide prevails, the deaths of children constitute no tragedy but rather a proper rite.

The basic conditions of events as stimulational factors must also be analyzed as conditions included in the total fields. What functions inhere in the objects to make it eligible for classification as tragical? Consider the cultural circumstances. When a person dies, there is the question whether to regard the death as a relief for the deceased after a prolonged serious illness, or for the relatives.

Numerous conditions attend the loss or destruction of some valued objects or conditions. The primary point here is to regard the event as a natural occurrence involving specific circumstances of a naturalistic sort. One may assume with considerable certainty that while all levels of social life may involve cataclysms, destruction, and loss, the socio-economic or general cultural conditions of the persons concerned in the situation exert great influence upon the total tragic situation.

In view of the preceding comments, it may be instructive to indicate some of the specific factors that are involved in and influence the occurrence of tragic events and their particular configuration. A suggestive list of factors in tragic situations is presented under the following categories.

Physiochemical Factors

Biological Factors

Societal Factors

Psychological Factors

Physiochemical Factors. Under this rubric, we place the many cosmic and terrestrial circumstances which affect the tragic circumstances of human personalities and groups. The emphasis, of course, is upon the losses and destruction which serve to cut off the potentialities for further development and advancement of persons and sets of persons. The effects may be of a major or minor intensity.

Biological Factors. Conditions of birth, maturation, and health are obviously important factors in anthropic tragic situations and correlate with lacerations, malformations, and malfunctions of various types. The damage may affect the victim or an onlooker who may be intimately related to the primary sufferer.

Societal Factors. This heading offers a convenient name for the many things and events which relate to persons in their homes and many societal environments. Relevant examples are the accidents of social class, such as the discrimination of minorities, foreigners, the poor, and women. Such factors operate effectively to erase available potentialities. Societal factors like economic impotency can even prevent the development of potentials in various directions.

Psychological Factors. Because psychology is concerned with the development of personality, it is richly equipped with factors which make for success and failure of individuals to cope with and adapt well or ill to ambient circumstances, including other persons, society in general, and the laws and customs of all varieties of governments, states, and political systems.

Individual personalities build up necessary or desirable traits and characteristics which may help or hinder in meeting the exigencies of daily living, and personal advancement.

PERIMETRIC VARIABLES OF TRAGIC FIELDS

Nothing happens without propitious circumstances. Setting factors are intimate and essential factors in all event fields. Among the setting factors we find outstanding spatiotemperality, pressure, concentration, temperature, and relativity, that is, the proximity and influence of other unit fields. Among the relational factors, chemical catalysis appears as extremely effective and strikingly prominent.

Since change is the essential variable in events, probably the most significant change is the curtailment of established potentiality, and this consequently merits the appelation of tragedy.

Abundant examples of large effects of setting factors exist in experimental investigations. To illustrate, in physics the set up of Davison and Germer demonstrates that light is undulating, while the experiment of A.H. Compton reveals a definite corpuscular nature. Perimetric factors include apparatus, hypotheses, experimental design, and many others.

A conspicuous example of the importance of setting factors in biological science is available in the progression from the abstractional study of anatomy, physiology, and pathology to the ecological branch and the investigation of the interbehavior of organisms with their surrounding things and events.

In psychology, we may quote a number of striking examples: (a) the color zoning of the retina by perimetric procedures which lost its validity by taking account of the light conditions; (b) the conclusion that the frontal lobes are the seat of the ability of animals to perform delayed reactions. Here too a change in light conditions negated the disability. These are only samples of a large number showing the effects of perimetric conditions. It is a reasonable inference that since values are concrete aspects of situations, they can easily and simply be variables in all types of tragic situations.

CHAPTER X

VALUE VARIABLES IN TRAGIC SITUATIONS

TRAGEDY STUDY IMPLIES VALUES

Problems of value invariably relate to all phases of tragedy study. This is the case despite the great divergences in view as to the nature and functions of values. It goes without saying that a consideration of the event continuum cannot avoid an interest in problems of quality, necessity, and fittingness when changes in the composition of event fields occur. Those whose premises are spiritistic or subjectivistic hold that values are of the essence of tragedy, both as authentic occurrences and as representations in theatrical plays. The following quotation indicates that,

> All that can be called tragic is contained within the realm of values and their relationships. In a universe free of values, such as that constructed by mechanical physics, there are no tragedies. Only where there is high and low, nobleman and peasant, is there anything like a tragic event.[1]

---

1. Scheler, M., "On the Tragic," in Abel, L. (ed.), *Moderns on Tragedy*, Greenwich, Fawcett, 1962, p. 252. Original entitled "Bemerkungen Zum Phänomen des Tragischen," in *Abhandlungen, und Aufsätze*, Erster Band, Leipzig, Weissen Bücher, 1915, p. 283.

Although the naturalistic view counters the notion that values are only anthropic, it does hold that values are features in most situations, including the formulation of theories, interpretations, and explanations concerning tragedy.

AMBIGUITIES CONCERNING VALUES

Because the values issue is so important for tragedy study, we consider briefly some errors concerning values and suggest corrections.

A. VALUES AS ABSTRACTIONS. To a great extent, values are regarded as simply abstractions, that is, preferred words. An example is the view that tragedy consists of a loss of value. This may be excusable only when dealing with general formulae, but not in descriptions of actual tragic events.

When one is interested in actual tragic events, the term "tragedy" must be applied only to concrete and specific components of authentic tragic situations. The specificity that is suggested here must address particular fields. Otherwise, descriptions and interpretations amount only to stilted and barren rhetoric.

In dramatic tragedies it must be specified what degree of value is attributable to the hero who is the protagonist. Also, the nature and significance of the loss or death of the hero protagonist should be specified. It is presumed, of course, that making values into entirely anthropic qualities is a restraining process when one is interested in the nature of tragedy as occurring events. It is not too farfetched to consider that the overemphasis of dramatic tragedy is pro facto reminiscent of a homocentric framework in which there is a dominating spiritistic factor derived from religious sources with a distinct deviance from factual circumstances.

B. VALUES AS PHASES OF EVENTS. Perhaps a more serious difficulty about values in tragedy study is an incorrect notion of their nature. Value analysis in the context of tragedy study brings to the fore philosophical attitudes as well as dramatic or literary criticism. From the standpoint of naturalistic philosophy or science, values may be nonanthropic. That is, value consists of some basic quality or property of objects. For some people, drugs possess virtues, that is, functions or consequences for certain purposes. It is a quality or virtue of metals or wood that they have qualities of durability and rigidity which make them valuable for certain circumstances. To continue with further examples, plants are valuable to constrain flowing water which prevents erosion. Various kinds of soil and clay substances are valuable for building materials and the production of vessels of various sorts. In the general conditions of nature, water is necessary material for the structures of animals and for the function of maintaining them. Similarly, bones are valuable for structure and strength so that all sorts of natural objects can exist in their particular environments.

C. VALUES AS EVALUATIONS. Writers on values frequently appear to operate under the influence of epistemological frameworks and thus interpret values as evaluations. In other words, they regard values as exclusively projections. Clearly, there are multiple errors in this view. First, it is in violent opposition to observation and scientific wisdom. Secondly, it runs counter to the facts of pristine values as they exist in everyday or technological situations, in the theatre, and in scientific studies.

VALUES IN THE EVENT CONTINUUM

For the better appreciation of values as variables or alleged values in tragical situations, it is advisable to analyze their traits in situations in the event continuum.

A. THEATRICAL SITUATIONS. Since plays are definitely constructive inventions, the rules of valid description seldom apply. For the most part, what are presumed to be values are merely arbitrary verbal projections. What are called values in theatrical displays usually are not values at all. Spurious values can be created by the manipulations of stage properties.

Probably the most impressive evidence of the ambiguity of literary tragedy are the numerous disagreements as to whether or not certain plays are truly tragedies. For example, Kaufmann[2] asserts that there is agreement that the following nine of Shakespeare's plays are tragedies: *Romeo and Juliet, Julius Caesar, Hamlet, Othello, King Lear, Macbeth, Antony and Cleopatra, Coriolanus,* and *Timon of Athens.* He would add *Richard III* and *Richard II* to make eleven altogether. But other writers are not so generous. The question of the number of Shakespeare's authentic tragedies is answered on the basis of the view the enumerator entertains about literary values and the general notion as to what constitutes the essence or vision concerning the tragic.

There is also the question as to the birth and death of tragedy. Did Euripides kill tragedy as Nietzsche[3] asserted or did it survive until, as Steiner wrote, "the tragic voice in drama is blurred or still."[4]

B. TECHNOLOGICAL SITUATIONS. Within the domain of technology, values as objective properties are most common. As we have mentioned above, any constructional activity, whether the making and using of tools to produce a building, master tool, or apparatus, or to build or demolish a house,

2. Kaufmann, W., *Tragedy and Philosophy,* Princeton, Princeton University Press, 1968, p. 317.
3. Nietzsche, F., *The Birth of Tragedy,* out of the Spirit of Music, W. Kaufmann (tr.), New York, Random House, 1967.
4. Steiner, G., *The Death of Tragedy,* New York, Knopf, 1961, p. 10.

requires stable and durable materials. Such facts throw considerable light on the problem of values whether in connection with tragical events or not.

C. SCIENTIFIC SITUATIONS. The nature of values from the standpoint of science is describable on various levels. In the first instance, on the qualities and other specifications of things or materials, for example, the malleability and rigidity useful for manipulation and service for the technological making of things. The second basis includes technical knowledge, prior experience, and style and custom. On the highest level stand the principles of the history and logic of science. Basically, the emphasis is upon a naturalistic treatment stemming from the conditions observed in actual practice and rational thinking.

HOW VALUES FIT INTO TRAGIC SITUATIONS

Values are always interrelated with tragic events because they have an existential range equal to that of most events. Values are factors in most situations and so constitute an authentic aspect of the event continuum. Certainly, values play an important part in aesthetic, economic, political, and ethical circumstances, though they are not excluded from the list of nonanthropic situations.

Values in tragic situations are specialized forms of events which are based on natural and cultural scales of various types. As we have suggested above, they must always be assumed to exist in specific situations and under special circumstances. So far as tragedy is concerned, the values that are lost or destroyed are potential in character. What adds to the description of tragedies or tragic situations is that attained abilities, capacities, expertise, and similar interbehavioral qualifications are lost or destroyed. It is not the mere death of a person that is tragical but the destruction or loss of patent possibilities. It is the demonstrated potentiality for growth and ability that usually makes death of a young person more tragic than the destruction or decline of a completely mature individual. In human situations, tragedy and its degree may stem from idiosyncratic judgments as well as from nonanthropic situations.

REFERENCES

Abel, L., *Metatheory,* New York, Hill and Wang, 1963.

Abel, L., "Is There a Tragic Sense of Life?" in Abel, L. (ed.), *Moderns on Tragedy,* Greenwich, Fawcett, 1967.

Anderson, M., *The Essence of Tragedy,* Washington, D.C., Anderson House, 1939.

Bradley, A.C., "Hegel's Theory of Tragedy" in *Oxford Lectures on Poetry,* (2), London, Macmillan, 1920.

Bradley, A.C., *Shakespearean Tragedy,* New York, St. Martin's, 1949.

Chaucer, G., *The Canterbury Tales,* W.W. Skeat (ed.), New York, Modern Library, 1929.

Chu, Kwang-Tsien, *The Psychology of Tragedy: A Critical Study of Various Theories of Tragic Pleasure,* Strasbourg, Librarie Universitaire de l'Universite, 1933.

Clay, J.H., "A New Theory of Tragedy: A Description and Evaluation," *Educational Theatre Journal,* VIII (1956), 295-305.

Courtney, W.L., *The Idea of Tragedy in Ancient and Modern Drama,* New York, Brentano's, 1900.

Delcourt, M., *Oedipe ou legend du conquerant,* Paris, Droz, 1944.

Freud, S., *Letters,* New York, Basic Books, 1954.

Frye, N., *Anatomy of Criticism,* Princeton, Princeton Univ. Press, 1957.

Green, A., *The Tragic Effect,* Cambridge, Cambridge Univ. Press, 1979.

Hegel, G.W.F., *Aesthetics,* T.M. Knox (tr.), (2), Oxford, Clarendon, 1975.

Hegel, G.W.F., *The Philosophy of Fine Arts,* F.P.B. Osmaston (ed.), (4), New York, Hacker Art Books, 1975.

Henn, T.R., The Harvest of Tragedy, London, Methuen, 1956.

Herder, J.F., *Adrastea,* Vol. 2, part 4, in *Sämmtliche Werke,* (23), Berlin, Werdmann, 1885.

Hume, D., "Of Tragedy" in *Essays,* London, Routledge, n.d.

Huzinga, J., *Homo Ludens: A Study of the Play Element in Culture,* London, Routledge, 1949.

Ibsen, H., *Little Eyolf,* Archer, W. (tr.), Chicago, Stone and Kimball, 1894.

Jaspers, K., *Tragedy is Not Enough,* London, Gollancz, 1953.

Jones, J., *On Aristotle and Greek Tragedy,* New York, Oxford, Univ. Press, 1962.

Kallen, H.M., "The Essence of Tragedy," *The International Journal of Ethics,* 1912, 17, 179-203.

Kantor, J.R., *The Logic of Modern Science,* Chicago, Principia, 1953.

Kantor, J.R., *Principles of Psychology,* Chicago, Principia, 1924, 1926.

Kantor, J.R., and Smith, N.W., *The Science of Psychology: An Interbehavioral Survey,* Chicago, Principia, 1975.

Kaufmann, W., *Philosophy and Tragedy,* Princeton, Princeton Univ. Press, 1968.

Kaufmann, W., *Tragedy and Philosophy,* Garden City, Doubleday, 1958.

Kermode, F., Foreword to Green, A., *The Tragic Effect,* Cambridge, Cambridge Univ. Press, 1979.

Kitto, H.D.F., *Poiesis, Structure and Thought,* Berkeley, Univ. Of California Press, 1966.

Krutch, J.W., Introduction to *Nine Plays by Eugene O'Neill,* New York, Modern Library, 1932.

Kuhns, R., *The House, the City and the Judge,* Indianapolis, Merrill, 1962.

Lacan, J., *Ecrits,* A. Sheridan (tr.), New York, Norton, 1977.

Lipps, T., *Der Streit uber die Tragödie,* Hamburg und Leipzig, 1891.

Lucas, F.L., *Tragedy,* New York, Harcourt Brace, 1928.

Lucas, F.L., *Tragedy in Relation to Aristotle's Poetics,* London, Hogarth, 1953.

McCollom, W.G., *Tragedy,* New York, Macmillan, 1957.

Mandel, O., *A Definition of Tragedy,* New York, New York Univ. Press, 1961.

Mann, O., *Poetik der tragödie,* Bern, Francke, 1958.

Michel, L. and Sewall, R.B. (eds.), *Tragedy: Modern Essays in Criticism,* Englewood Cliffs, N.J., Prentice-Hall, 1963.

Muller, H.J., *The Spirit of Tragedy,* New York, Knopf, 1956.

Myers, H.A., *Tragedy: A View of Life,* Ithaca, Cornell Univ. Press, 1956.

Nietzsche, F., The Birth of Tragedy, W. Kaufmann (tr.), New York, Vintage, 1967.

O'Connor, W. Van, *Climates of Tragedy,* Baton Rouge, Louisiana State Univ. Press, 1943.

Philipson, M.H., "Some Reflections on Tragedy," *Journal of Philosophy,* LV (1958), 197-203.

Raphael, D.D., *The Paradox of Tragedy,* London, Allen and Unwin, 1960.

Richards, I.A., *Principles of Literary Criticism,* New York, Harcourt, Brace, 1926.

Ross, W.D. (ed.), *The Student's Oxford Aristotle,* Vol. 6, 1449^{b}, 23.

Schiller, F., *Uber Den Grund Des Vergnügens an Tragischen Gegenständen,* and *Uber Die Tragische Kunst,* in *Sämtliche Werke,* (13), Stuttgart and Berlin, Cotta'sche Bibliothek, n.d.

Schopenhauer, A., *The World As Will And Idea,* Haldane and Kemp (trs.), (6), London, Kegan Paul, 1907.

Sewall, R.B., *The Vision of Tragedy,* new ed., New Haven, Yale, 1980.

Shakespeare, W., *Coriolanus, King Lear, Macbeth, Othello, Richard II, Romeo and Juliet.*

Smart, J.S., "Tragedy," *Essays and Studies By Members of English Association,* VIII, Oxford, Oxford Univ. Press, 1922, 9-36.

Steiner, G., *The Death of Tragedy,* New York, Knopf, 1961.

Volkelt, J., *Ästhetik Des Tragischen,* (2) Munich, Beck, 1906.

Wheeler, L.P., *Josiah Willard Gibbs: The history of a great mind,* New Haven, Yale University Press, 1951.

Winnicott, D.W., *Playing and Reality,* London, Tavistock, 1971.

Wolf, T.H., "A New Perspective on Alfred Binet: Dramatist of Le Theatre de L'Horreur," *Psychological Record,* 1982, 32, 397-407.

Wyckoff, E., *The Complete Greek Tragedies,* Chicago, Univ. of Chicago Press.

EPILOGUE

THE LAST CHANCE

Not only is man mortal, but if he is sensitive to social proprieties, he is also apologetic because of his fallibilities. If he is an author, he wants his writings to be clear in the hope of fair appraisal, whether approval or judicious rejection. That explains this epilogue, the last chance an author has to present his findings and his interpretations. The present writer adopts the particular method of abstracting each chapter with relevant comments. The coverage is as complete as time, space, and current circumstances allow.

PREFACE

BASIC ASSUMPTIONS. At the outset, the writer declares forcefully that tragic events are items in the event continuum. All the events of the continuum are presumed to be natural happenings, which includes the evolution of all things and events including hominids, their societies, and institutions. In accordance with this view, the writer believes that tragedy or tragic events can be effectively studied when identified as occurring on each of three levels of the continuum. The nature of each level or type is suggested by the following categorization.

(a) Tragedy as momentous events in nature;

(b) Tragedy as unique human events;

(c) Tragedy as representation of human circumstances.

In the event continuum, tragic events parallel events of many other types. Each event consists of (1) a particular composition or structure, (2) behavior, and (3) conditions. Precise and exact knowledge of any level or type and its variation from the others requires the ascertainment of a number of factors.

SCIENTIFIC APPROACH. The author states decisively that the present investigation conforms strictly to scientific standards. That signifies the observation of events and their description and interpretation. As guidelines are proffered: (a) the principle of specificity, and (b) the principle of total relevant factors as indicated in the text.

CHAPTER I

TRAGEDY AS EVENTS AND AS DRAMATIC DEPICTION

At the very threshold of tragedy study, a distinction must be made between (a) tragic events as unique occurrences in the event continuum and (b) the compositions commonly known as literary tragedies. Aside from the semantic problem suggested here, there is the need for precise differentiation between the different phases of tragedy in order to ascertain the basic nature of tragic events. Such a differentiation depends, of course, upon the variant composition of tragic events. In this chapter is proposed a distinct three-fold variation of events as follows.

1. Pristine or inorganic events

2. Organismic events

3. Literary compositions

EVENTS OBSERVED OR INTERPRETED

A most important distinction to be respected by students of tragic events is that between (a) tragic situations of whatever type, and (b) the attitudes and other reactions to the items observed. Care must be taken not to identify beliefs and descriptions with the events themselves. This confusion spells the doom of (a) any investigation of a pristine object or event, or (b) criticism of a play.

But granting the separation of attitudes or other reactions to tragic events, judgments about the events are better when due care is taken to observe the standpoint and discipline in which one is interested. In this chapter, the following five approaches to tragic events are listed and characterized.

1. Literary criticism
2. Philosophical perspectives
3. Moral standpoints
4. Religious institutions
5. Psychological circumstances

Throughout all the various approaches we discern the influence of the improper background and foreground of the spiritistic culture. That influence is manifested in the attitudes of the workers in various disciplines concerned with tragic events. Tragic events are treated with questionable views concerning humankind and hominid societies. Souls, spirits, and minds are assumed to be existences beyond the words used in discourse about them.

CHAPTER II

POSTULATES FOR THE STUDY OF TRAGEDY

A fairly late but excellent development in the scientific domain is the postulative alertness to make certain what premises influence observations, analyses, and other aspects of investigation. An instructive illustration is the declaration that an antimentalistic view of psychology has no place for behavior like thinking, reasoning, and remembering because such performances are regarded as spiritistic. Overlooked is the fact that such behaviors, like all psychological activities, are acts of persons in reciprocal interbehavior with what psychologists call stimulus objects and conditions.

As to the pertinent postulates of this work, great emphasis is placed upon the following assumptions.

NATURALISTIC POSTULATE. The naturalistic assumption holds that whatever exists or happens constitutes a unique and autonomous event. What are excluded are transcendental creators and creations. All human creations are clearly the transformation of previously existing materials. Nonhuman novelties are products of changes which bring about variations in elements or total fields on the basis of actual conditions such as temperature, mass, pressure, movements, and so on.

POSTULATE OF EVOLUTION. Things and events are all developed on the basis of prior elements and conditions.

POSTULATE OF ANALYSIS. Scientific work requires intense alertness to the distinction between (a) things and events, and (b) the descriptions and interpretations placed upon them.

The primary point is the realization that objects such as pristine things and events preexist the subsequent event of persons interacting with them and that plays are constructions so that the composers and their conditions and backgrounds must be taken into account.

LINGUISTIC POSTULATE. An important assumption in tragedy study hinges upon the ambiguities and limitations of speech and verbal formulae. A prime example is the word "tragedy" which permits the confusion between (a) tragic events as natural happenings with (b) all sorts of literary productions. For precise references to the various things and events in the event continuum, a much larger vocabulary is needed than is actually available.

CHAPTER III

HISTORICAL SUCCESSION OF TRAGEDY STUDY

Instructive for the study of tragedy study is the time or period perspective. Three such periods are designated by the following names, (a) Objective Greek period, (b) Post Greek Spiritistic period, and (c) Current Objective period. Each is characterized from a scientific point of view and classified as to objectivity and subjectivity, as also from the standpoint of (a) literary production and (b) events of nature. In this chapter, tragedy in the theatre is traced forward from the work of (a) Aristotle, (b) through the classical subjective cycle to (c) the current objective period.

CHAPTER IV

TRAGEDY IN SPIRITISTIC CONVERSION

Coincident with the cultural deterioration of the objective view of the classical period, the era of subjectivity and spiritism set in to continue until the present. The present chapter then is devoted to the consideration of a number of slightly varying spiritistic approaches to the problems of literary tragedy. These are revealed in the form of definitions. These definitions of tragedy are supplemented by similar definitions of conventional philosophers.

CHAPTER V

THE EVENT CONTINUUM

At the background of a naturalistic and scientific approach to tragedy study stands the event continuum. Tragic events in every form as well as the tragedies of literature are localized at some specific point in the massive flow of happenings. However, not all scholars accept the consequences of such a naturalistic viewpoint. For this reason, this chapter is primarily concerned with the impact of philosophical and psychological views concerning tragedy as occurring events, both of events in nature and in general human circumstances. It is understood, of course, that most conventional philosophers postulate that all events of the continuum are spiritistic projections and not independently existing entities. Such subjectivistic views contrast radically with the naturalistic postulates of the present work.

In this chapter, too, is considered the very important issue for tragedy study of the nature and relation of potential and completely actualized events. According to naturalistic philosophy and psychology, all occurring event fields exist as potential and actualized phases. Every occurring event exists first in potentia, that is, the elements of event fields may not be in full convergence. Once the essential elements are all conjoined, the field is complete and the event takes place as an entirely actualized feature of the event continuum in continuity with all other actualized events, whether inorganic, organismic, or hominid.

The primary physiochemical example of potentiality advancing to actualization is the general process of catalysis.

An illustration is found in the story of the development of Ringers solution. It seems that Ringer attempted for many months to produce a solution by using only NaCl and KCl without success until his assistant used tap water instead of distilled water which brought in calcium ions, and produced a satisfactory solution.[1]

As the text indicates, tragedy is definable as the truncation or interference with the actualization of significant potentiality.

CHAPTER VI

TRUNCATED POTENTIALITY HYPOTHESIS ILLUSTRATED

Although examples of tragic events do not prove the naturalistic hypothesis, they add considerable credibility to it. This chapter presents illustrations of the truncation of potentiality gleaned from literary sources as well as from general life conditions. It is, of course, assumed that since the selection of illustrations involves interpretation, the way is open for individual differences and dissonant judgments, still, the illustrations offered lend considerable expository support to the general hypothesis.

CHAPTER VII

SEMANTIC COMPLICATIONS IN TRAGEDY STUDY

The study of tragedy, like all investigations, is involved with linguistic complications. Semantic problems may greatly hamper attempts at exposition and intercommunication since language or speech consists of constructions. Specifically, the

1. Baldwin, E., *The Nature of Biochemistry*, Cambridge, Cambridge Univ. Press, 1967, p. 6.

language or its unit terms may not actually refer to the things or conditions supposedly referred to.

With respect to tragic events, there are three circumstances that result in semantic errors. They are (1) inadequate philosophical and psychological premises in the approach to events, (2) entanglements in everyday vocabulary, and (3) the term "tragedy" may be restricted to literary affairs and not general tragic events.

Because of the above circumstances, the seventh chapter includes a brief scientific excursus into the linguistic domain. An attempt is made to elucidate the influence of word usage and the uncritical naming process in treating tragedy and tragical events.

It is assumed that critical attention to semantic and other phases of speech and language will cast some light on the general subject of tragic events.

CHAPTER VIII

PSYCHOLOGICAL ASPECTS OF TRAGIC EVENTS

Although anthropic tragedy is one of two types, it really dominates the entire domain of tragedy study. Hence, human situations are always thoroughly interpenetrated with psychological issues. Now since the present work is pitched on a scientific level, it can be supported only by a scientific version of psychology. Thus, Chapter Eight proposes a brief exposition of scientific psychology.

As the text has indicated, the literature of tragedy is replete with theories that can only be classified as transcendental. Critics of literary tragic situations tolerate the presence in plays of fate, ghosts, witches, and similar counterexperiential entities as also other impossible and fanciful inventions. Scientific psychology serves to put a quietus to such erroneous presentations of presumable human events.

Consequently, comparison is made between various transcendent models of psychology and one constructed on observable and scientific lines. Furthermore, the scholarly service rendered by a rational model results in the building of a general satisfactory viewpoint as well as bringing about improvements in the treatment of specific tragedy issues.

CHAPTER IX

MULTIVARIATE CONDITIONS INVOLVED IN TRAGIC EVENTS

No naturalistic description of events can be adequate without specifying the conditions under which it occurs. Only in this way can one expect properly to understand the core element of tragic changes- the interference with actualization of potentialities. Especially important is the knowledge of accompanying conditions when the tragic continuum embraces two such types of tragedy as the nonanthropic and the anthropic.

The writer proposes that sufficient evidence is available with respect to conditions to warrant the hypothesis that a definite continuity exists in the event continuum joining tragic circumstances of nonanthropic and anthropic types as also lending credibility to the general hypothesis.

CHAPTER X

VALUE VARIABLES IN TRAGIC SITUATIONS

Tragic events, no less than any complex anthropic situation, are heavily fraught with value factors. It is, then, an important task to analyze situations to ascertain at what point value variables are situated, plus their formula of quantity or intensity, plus their effect upon the total event field.

The constant presence of values in all situations and their patent importance demands at least a brief analysis and evaluation of the nature and operation of values. In Chapter Ten, consideration is accorded some ambiguities and errors concerning values and a method of overcoming unsatisfactory assessments.

From a scientific point of view, the term "value" refers to a property or characteristic of things, persons, or situations which naturally coordinates with other properties of things such as solidity or fluidity of material, reliability of persons, or the circumstances surrounding the evaluating processes.

In the context of tragedy investigation, the weight of the value variables in event situations serve to give persons, things, or conditions a scale rating as either tragic, pitiful, usual, or unusual.

NAME INDEX

SUBJECT INDEX